JOBLESS

$10K A MONTH EARNER

A REALISTIC APPROACH AND PRACTICAL SOLUTIONS

JOHN CHRISTOPHER

REPROGRAM MY MIND PUBLISHING
Washington, D.C.

Jobless
$10K A Month Earner
A Realistic Approach and Practical Solutions

www.ReprogramMyMind.com

Copyright ©2023 by John Christopher

DEDICATION

To my children- may you dream big, reach high, and always believe in the limitless possibilities that lie ahead. Your curiosity, creativity, and boundless energy inspire me to build a world where every idea has the power to flourish.

As you continue to grow, may you discover the joy of learning, the resilience to overcome challenges, and the kindness to share your success with others.

Here's to a future filled with endless opportunities and the belief that, with determination and a curious spirit, you can achieve anything. Pursue your passions, overcome obstacles, and embrace the endless possibilities that you can create.

TABLE OF CONTENTS

PART 1 - LET'S GET STARTED

PART 2 - HOW TO EARN INCOME ONLINE

PART 3

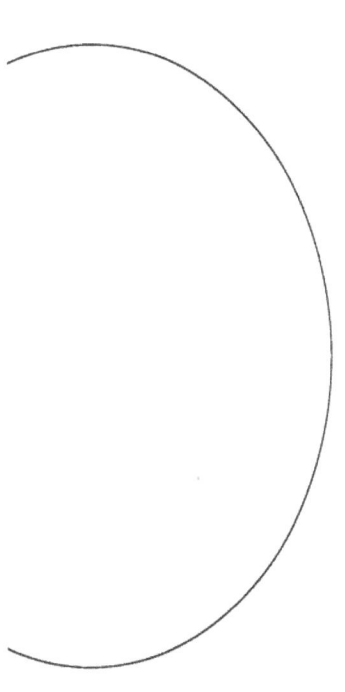

THE INTRODUCTION

DISCLAIMERS

I do not hold any certifications as a financial advisor or human resources professional. Any action that you take based on the information in this book is solely your decision and the results are solely your own. (My attorney told me to say all of that but still, I stand by these statements.) The advice I give to you throughout this book is from three resources: (1) my education which includes my bachelors in Business Administration and my Masters in Business Administration with a concentration in financial systems; (2) my personal experience in some manner with every one of these industries mentioned in this book; and (3) extensive and intensive research.

Also, please know that everything in this book you can find online for free. All I did was compile the information into an easy-to-read book plus offer my personal and professional insight, and some strategy so that you get the truth, learn the secrets (well, they're not really secrets), and get educated to become an online earner while still working your regular 9 to 5.

I am in no way guaranteeing that you can succeed in any venture discussed in this book. However, all circumstances are based on your individual effort and personal choices. As the saying goes, you get out what you put in. It's all about your efforts, your efficiency and the system you create.

PART 1

Let's Get Started

START

HOW TO READ THIS BOOK

This book is written for your personal use. It will help you structure a "business system" so that you can thrive at earning money online while still working your regular 9 to 5 job (if you have one) or creating an entire career for yourself from home or remotely. This book also includes initially non-online opportunities but that relate to online (or automated) structures. The book is written in an easy-to-read format that allows you to skim and easily locate the necessary sections and topics for a quick review.

This next statement you must make note of- there is so very much connecting knowledge all throughout this book and I note it at times. You will see how much all of the concepts in this book relate and how using information from one section will help with other sections. I encourage you to highlight specific parts that you feel are beneficial or if you're listening, take notes!

I use tables in some sections to demonstrate the quality of each topic and the earning potential as well as the difficultly level. Keep in mind that not all of the topics are easy or have the highest earning potential. Through the book, I do my best to be as realistic as possible and explain the ins and outs of how to utilize each venture to maximize your personal success. Please note that all factors/scores are my opinion and based on my experiences, knowledge and expertise and not intended to be used as a final matrix or measurement for your success in delivering the services or products within the topic/section. You might find yourself so successful that you dispel my scores!

Please pay close attention to the below information because I use these abbreviations throughout this book. Use the legend below to help you identify each abbreviation and its meaning.

Let's take a quick look at some of the abbreviations that will be used throughout this book and the explanations of them here:

- DL – Difficulty Level
- REP – Realistic Earning Potential
- MI – Monetary Investment
- PTC - Personal or Potential Time Commitment
- SMS – Suggested Marketing Structure

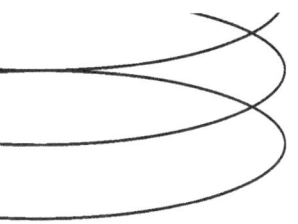

DL – Difficulty Level

Difficulty is rated between 1 – 5 with 1 being least difficult and 5 being the most difficult. Some topics will have less or more difficulty depending on a vast array of factors. For example, if you choose a business venture that requires you to have a following on social media, the level of difficulty can be based on the number of followers that you need to have success pitching or selling products outside of your immediate sphere of influence.

Difficulty levels are based on 3 factors:

1. How fast can you earn money or how long will it take to earn money using this particular method?
2. What is the entry barrier or difficulty entering this market?
3. How competitive is the market for this service i.e., is the market saturated with people doing the same thing?

Let's look at a quick example:

Network Level Marketing (Note: I chose network level marketing because it's not mentioned in this book). I will grade each factor and then come up with the final difficulty level.

FACTOR	GRADE
1. How fast can you earn money or how long will it take to earn money using this particular method?	3.5
2. What is the entry barrier or difficulty entering this market?	2.5
3. How competitive is the market for this service, i.e., is the market saturated with people doing the same thing?	4.0
TOTAL SCORE	10/3 =
FINAL AVERAGE GRADE (Difficulty Level – DL)	3.35 rd.

REP – Realistic Earning Potential

The Realistic Earning Potential is based on an earning potential perspective of what you can actually earn with each service, product, etc. Using a mathematically realistic approach, I factor the REP based on what you will actually earn per transaction. Using the network level marketing example from above, the realistic earning potential will always have a range between two numbers. For example, for network marketing, the earning potential is from $25 – $1000 per transaction depending on the service or products you are selling.

MI – Monetary Investment

Let's be honest, many of the services and products offered within this book will require some sort of monetary investment. This investment can range from the utilization of your own car (gas, wear and tear) or technology that you may have or may need to upgrade, to an upfront annual fee or monthly recurring fee. However, I did my best to include services that are free. Where there are fees associated with start-up, I absolutely note this. Again, because I have written this book for those that are currently working a job and are starting from scratch in a new industry, I adopted a methodology that serves to answer questions such as:

- Is there an entry fee?
- Are there any marketing fees that would be necessary?
- Are there any additional or miscellaneous fees that may occur or are recurring, for example, insurance, state or local taxes, legal fees, etc.

Instead of offering a mathematical calculated number, I utilized the methodology above to provide you with three ranges to keep this simple:

- Minimal
- Medium
- High

PTC - Personal or Potential Time Commitment

Personal or Potential Time Commitment is self-explanatory. Ultimately the time spent on your external or "side hustles" can greatly depend on you and your personal circumstances such as school, children, church, work, dates, social life and so on. In essence, the PTC is really just the estimated or recommended time needed to ensure a successful movement of products/services to generate income in a realistic manner.

Using my experience as an example, I initially spent about 3-6 hours a day doing the following for one of my projects: researching the best products and services to sell; putting together the best grassroots ad or social media post campaigns; actually running the test; restructuring the post based on insights; and then reposting. Remember, this was just for one project and essentially just for one advertisement. Your time spent will vary based on your current life choices and outside commitments. As a key note and since I'm being realistic, you will need to sacrifice something in order for this to really work.

SMS – Suggested Marketing Structure

Because marketing of any business can be quite robust, I cover marketing in depth in another book and video series. However, in this book I provide solid marketing strategies for you that will work. There are only two types of marketing structures I suggest and these are based on structures I have proven will work effectively. These two structures are:

- Grassroots – basically free campaigns or methods for advertising or marketing products/services.
- Paid – paid ads or services

As you review the topics in this book and all of our Qualifying Factors please do your research to determine if a particular marketing strategy is logical for the topic you choose to pursue.

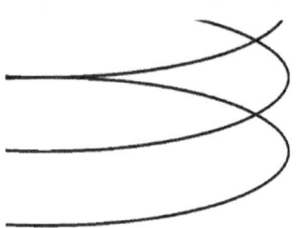

Qualifying Factors Example:

Each section or topic will start with a table like in Figure 1 below.

QUALIFYING FACTORS	GRADE
Difficulty Level (DL)	2.5
Realistic Earning Potential (REP)	$1 – 100 Per Day
Monetary Investment (MI)	Minimal
Potential Time Commitment (PTC)	1 – 4 hr/per/day
Suggested Marketing Structure (SMS)	Grassroots, Paid or Both

Figure 1

After I provide to you the Qualifying Factors, I will define what the topic is and give you some important aspects to know about the topic's industry. I will then provide the pros and cons of the topic or the pros and cons of the specific websites for you to get started, or pros and cons on both of these areas.

All of the information in each section will provide you more than enough background and an adequate foundational knowledge for you to make an informed decision as to whether or not this particular venture is one that you want to pursue in order to add to or replace your current income source(s).

SHOULD I BUY AN ONLINE COURSE

Yes and No. Be careful. There are thousands of people selling online courses, books, products and services that will tell you how you can make a lot of money with very little effort and in a short amount of time. They claim "all you have to do is..." and you can make thousands of dollars just like that.

Here's a fact - there are some legit programs, courses, books, mentors, and online help forums that are worth paying for or at least worth paying something for. However, you have to weed out the scammers, the fakers and the greedy money chasers. How do you do this? Keep reading.

First of all, **NEVER CHASE MONEY.** When you pay for some of these online courses or even pay to be a part of a social media "closed" group (yes, this is real), you are basically chasing money. My desire is that you take the knowledge contained in this book and create a "system" that causes money to be attracted to you. I will get into building a money attraction system later in this book but for now, chasing money is like chasing that girl or guy that does not really want you or like you. You may get some attention for a short period of time, but eventually that girl/guy is going to walk away from the relationship because you keep chasing them. Do not chase the money. You have to find a way to make money attracted to you.

THE HARD CORE TRUTH

Here are the facts, the tough love and honest points that some of these so called "gurus" providing these courses and groups might not tell you:

- This "make money online" market is extremely crowded and saturated with people trying to do the same exact thing. However, these are still billion dollar industries and earning $5K to $10K or more a month is absolutely very realistic.
- These gurus earn their money selling you or others the course, not necessarily doing or practicing what they preach.

- Many of the top earners in this business are influencers or individuals that have large followings.

- If you do not already have at least 1000 followers on at least 1 social media platform (YouTube, Instagram, etc.), you will need to work to grow your number of followers (you may have to do paid ads to grow your audience).

- You will need to work additional hours in addition to your 9 to 5 hours in order to really make this work and consistently earn $5K or more a month (average 3 – 6 extra work hours day). *You can also build a system that results in automated sales.*

- You will get discouraged, frustrated and be confused at times. Why? Because some stuff will not work and some stuff will work. Go with what works. My saying is *Trial and Error, Learn from Failure*

- You must conduct research and possibly have to learn a new skill (e.g. video editing, website design, etc.). If you decide to pay for a course, learn from the top earners that are already succeeding in what you are looking to do. Take time to learn new and valuable skills.

- Invest in yourself by identifying a mentor. A good mentor is someone that is trustworthy and someone that you can actually talk with via a phone call as opposed to only email or the dreaded DMs. Most importantly, a good mentor is someone who has a proven track record at success in the area in which you are looking to also be a success.

- You will need to personally test at least 2-3% of the products and services that you are trying to sell. You do not want to offer a product or service for which you would not even appreciate paying money. Make sure you know what you are selling.

- You will face uncertainty, fear of success or fear of failure, or negative feedback from friends, family and even people you do not know on your social media feeds. Don't give up, don't quit. Stay strong minded and have a strong mindset.

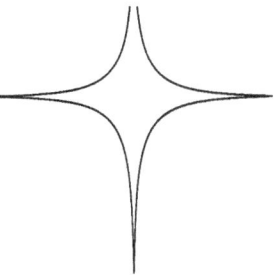

Forget everything you just read from above... unless... Why? Because, unless you have the proper mindset, this entire book will be a waste of YOUR time and money. If your mindset is not open, this book along with any other self-help books you read will go into one ear and out the other with no real action. If you believe you are going to fail, then that's exactly what will happen. On the flip side, if you believe you are going to succeed, then guess what – YOU WILL SUCCED. In order for your mindset to change, you may have to unlearn some things or change some behaviors.

For example, growing up my parents taught me to go to college, get a degree and then get a job. They did not teach me anything about entrepreneurship. As a result, I had to unlearn the behavior of thinking that a physical brick and mortar job is the only way to earn a secure income with benefits. The question becomes, how does one really change their mindset? Well, let's start this way - your mindset can be developed in the following sequence:

RESEARCH - LEARN - REPEAT - INITIATION - ACTION - BEHAVIOR - BECOMING

In anything you do, you must first conduct the research to properly learn what you will need. The more you repeat your learning, the more you understand what steps to initiate. Take the steps that work and make it a practicing part of your knowledge. Your practices become your actionable tasks. Once you have taken some action on a consistent basis, these actions become part of your behavior and ultimately your state of being.

For example, when you were a child, you had to learn a set of skills or concepts in order to pass to the next grade level such as multiplication tables. With each grade level there was always some repetition or review of concepts around multiplication tables you learned the year before. Then over time, you memorized those concepts and because of that consistent review and doing the practice problems that involved multiplication tables, it became a part of your behavior to know them easily. You could say that you had become good at being able to answer multiplication problems. You learn that 2 x 2 will always equal 4. Now take into consideration the reverse situation where, hypothetically, a child had been taught that 2 x 2 is equal to 4.1. Well, of course over time when that child became an adult, it would be difficult to teach it differently that 2 x 2 actually equals 4.

Mindsets work the same way. Even though you have been taught one way for so many years, you sometimes have to conduct the research to understand something is accurate or true and then learn that concept. Then repeat the learning of it by initiating the steps to practice it and then act on those steps by doing the steps. This ultimately develops into your behavior that becomes part of you being in the state of the mindset you need to be truly successful.

INVESTING YOUR MONEY AND TIME

Let me share a something I heard some time ago:

"The difference between poor, middle class and the wealthy is not how much money they make. And it's not even how much money they have. The real difference between these classes of people is what they believe the purpose of money to be. For example, the mindset of the poor believes the purpose of money is to pay bills. So the only reason they go to work every day is to get paid on a specific schedule and then hand the money over to someone else to pay a bill. The middle class mindset believes the purpose of money is the establish good credit so that they can buy things they really can't afford, pay them off over time and indulge in occasional niceties [and pay bills]. The wealthy mindset understands the primary purpose of money is to turn it into more money or "create" or "cause" money to be attracted to them."

Unknown

In other words, don't be afraid to invest your money to earn more money. Another perspective says, 99% of businesses do not need capital in order to get started. And still another perspective defines an entrepreneur as one who starts their business with other people's money (that is, investors). Most businesses can be started with very little or no capital at all. Let's be very clear- in most instances, it does take money to earn more money. That doesn't mean that you can't earn additional income by utilizing grassroots (free based) strategies. With many of the services and products in this book, you don't need any money to get started. However, you may need some money to market the products and services you're selling unless you already have the platform with the adequate number of followers.

Why do you need followers? First, it makes it easier for you to sell online services and products to your community. (Strategy.) For example, when I first started selling online, I didn't have any following. So I had to budget my job salary in order to run ads on Instagram, Facebook and YouTube to get both followers/likes and ads to sell my products. In the beginning I had no clue about running ads so I conducted a ton of online research about running effective social media ads. In the meantime, I decided to take a remote job with flexible hours, use that money to fund marketing campaigns and grow my audience (4 hours a day). See how that works? See the strategy? That's only one approach. In this book I give you several approaches to a strategic but honest, truthful and secure way of earning additional income.

Time - another facet that most people don't immediately understand. Your time spent is indeed money. Not only is time money, in some cases you may need to sacrifice your time and invest some money in order to make this work. Using the example above, I worked from home, or remote job, that paid me about $22 an hour and I worked about 2 – 4 extra hours a day and got paid biweekly. After taxes, I brought in about $380 a week. I invested a small portion of that biweekly salary to take a online course on Udemy (time) on video editing. Then I paid for a royalty free license to use footage (istockphoto.com) and created videos (time) to use as social media ads. Guess what? Not every ad I ran worked. I still didn't earn my money back off quite a few of my starting ad campaigns and as a result, I had to go back and redo the videos to make them more interesting and compelling, then pay for additional ad campaigns.

Not every situation will be like this. Some individuals find easier ways and/or have the creative talent to make grassroots or paid video ads much more attractive the first go-round. The point is that eventually you will need to invest time and money into not only yourself, but also your business.

SAVING MONEY - A PERSPECTIVE

I am not going to dive too deep into this topic because there are so many perspectives on personal financial budgets. It is ultimately up to you, your circumstances and situation on how you assess and utilize the concepts I mention. I am only going to offer one perspective and then give you some mathematical support as evidence of its logical approach. Ready?

Don't save money and don't put your money into regular popular banks. WOW! You were probably not ready for that. And I may get some heat for putting forth such a statement. What if I told you to pull ALL of your money out of banks like Bank of America, Wells Fargo, PNC, etc.? Why? The average interest rate on a savings or money market account is .01% to 3% Annual Percentage Yeild (APY). If I try to save $5000 in a savings account with 1% APY interest, assuming I don't withdraw any money for an entire year:

$5000 at 1% APY compounded for 12 months = 50.23.

So in order to earn money on my money, I need to let it sit in the regular bank for 12 months and only get $50??? That doesn't seem fair. And not only should you pull your money out of these types of accounts but also out of the checking accounts as well. Instead, open a brokerage account. Brokerage accounts are savings/checking accounts that allow you to invest in various types of stocks, EFTs and other investment vehicles that will earn you more interest on your money than a regular savings account. You can also still have ATM and debit card access with these types of accounts.

Instead of saving your money, use the money that you're willing to save and purchase monthly dividend stocks or invest in assets or vehicles that pay out monthly. Invest in controllable, easy to liquidate investment vehicles. I touch a little bit more on this topic in *Section 4 Monthly Dividend Stocks.*

Let's look at a mathematical approach using that same $5000.

Let's purchase 500 shares of company XYZ at $10 per share that pays out a monthly dividend of 0.25 cents per share. That will be 0.25 per month per share on the 500 shares that you own. Now let's multiply that 0.25 cents by your 500 shares and that equals $125 per month. Now you see the difference. Therefore, don't save your money but invest your money.

Here's the other important part of this concept. Since bills have to be paid, you must consider investing like a bill. Most of your bills are paid monthly, I would guess. So make investments a monthly bill. Investing or putting money into an investment account must be like paying your electric bill or cell phone bill. If you view investing like a bill, your financial outlook will greatly improve.

BUILDING A FOLLOWING

Building a following is an entire book and topic by itself. I will provide you with some of the best tips and tricks to build a following that I personally know about. However, because of the depth and breadth of this subject, there is no way I can cover every facet in this book. You have best selling authors that specialize in writing books about building a following. After reading this book, and if you don't already have the following you need, I recommend reading the following books:

- *Influencer*, Brittany Hennessy

- *Content Mavericks: How to Grow Your Business With Insanely Shareable Content*, Andrew Pickering and Peter Gartland

- *Top of Mind: Use Content to Unleash Your Influence and Engage Those Who Matter To You*, John Hall

Building a following is very important when using online methods like affiliate marketing or Amazon affiliates, Udemy, and nearly all of the sections discussed in this book. The truth is those with a healthy social media following are the top earners when it comes to earning money online.

In order to build a following, you need these key aspects:

1. A Strategy
2. Quality and Sharable and Consistent Content

A Strategy - You will need a strategy to build a following. The below strategy on building a following is just one example. Use this information to tailor your own strategy on building your following. You may find that you will have to reformat portions of your strategy to maximize what works.

There are two different types of general audience building techniques on social media platforms:

- Organic – Building a following "from scratch" or from others sharing and resharing your content and then following you, your page, creating groups, social clubs, etc.
- Paid – Using paid ad structures to get people to like your posts and like and follow your page.

Quality Content – The quality of your content and it's shareability is key. What does this mean? This means that if you can create content that other people are willing to share then you can create a following or your posts can go viral. Look at some examples of content that catches your attention and note what made you stay tuned for longer than five seconds. For example, have you ever seen an advertisement to adopt a pet or donate to children in need living in harsh conditions? Those ads are designed to tug at your emotional heart strings. The best content deliverers know this one key concept- know your audience!

Consistent Content - Even if you use a paid strategy to build your audience, you still need to deliver quality (shareable) content at least once a week and you may want to post more often depending on the circumstances. For example, if you are drop shipping items that are related to Valentine's Day and today is February 7th, you would need to post quality shareable content at least three times before Valentine's Day. A once-a-week posting strategy will not work here.

First, you must understand that each social media platform has its own types of audiences. For example, in the United States, roughly 77% of people between the ages of 30-49 use Facebook. Roughly 67% of people ages 18-29 use Instagram.

To give you further clarity, I will share my personal strategy as an example of how I was able to build my following.

I personally used a combination of both organic and paid strategies to build my audience. Even if you use a paid strategy to build your audience, you still need to deliver quality content and consistently; at least once a week. There are several social media sites. For the purposes of this book, I will just use the 4 of them which are Facebook, Instagram, YouTube and TicTok. For me, for starters, I mainly used Facebook and figuring out how to cross those other platforms with creative and sharable content was my task.

Right now, I have over 4000 followers on my personal Facebook page. To be perfectly honest, I probably don't know more than 150 of them if not less. I was able to generate that many so-called FB friends because I'm also a real estate investor, youth football coach, day trader and crypto trader and have been in several networking groups related to each of those topics. So over a few years, I have accepted random people's friend requests (although I would not recommend that) and even sent random people friend requests within these networks.

At first I noticed that only certain posts got likes or comments. For example, if I posted pictures of myself, my children or something personal about me or my family, I would get a ton of responses or comments, mainly from people that know me personally and maybe a few strangers. However, if I posted something random like a quote about money or business or a post that tried to sell something, it was like I could hear the crickets chirping. No responses. Why was this? First of all, I totally get the social media algorithms and which posts friends see and from which friends, etc.

That fact aside, I realized that those posts were not relatable or tugged at their emotions or interests. Those posts did not include that quality content as discussed above. Further, I was not posting that quality content on a consistent basis.

Therefore, the next part of my strategy was to break down my followers into these 4 categories:

- Family or Friend - friends I knew from work, school, personal family members, personal friends.
- Real estate friends – those in the RE market in some way.
- Crypto friends – those that trade in crypto.
- Youth football friends – those that have children in or coach youth sports, etc.

Once I realized my categories, I could better tailor my posts and target my audience (remember, know your audience!). I'll use family as my example in one of my first targeted posts. Because I knew this category of my friends list would only respond to personal posts with pictures of me and my children, posts about my travel or on vacation, or some personal accomplishment, I started to create content that resonated with them. These posts also appealed to friends in other categories so I made sure to note these occurrences. Here's one of my post examples.

> "SMH As I'm headed to @SevenSpringsSkiResort I just realized I forgot my charger cord. I tell you these little portable travel chargers are right on time and so convenient. https://amzn.to/3QctBoD If you like traveling, I highly recommend keeping one of these in your car. #HavingFunInTheSnow #WinterSkiSeason"

Of course that Amazon link is my affiliate link and I included pictures of myself and the actual product. Notice how I appealed to my friends and family. I know they love traveling – always posting pictures of themselves being on vacations, checking in at special locations and even sharing their food pictures every once in a while. Get the point? I'm traveling, it's a personal picture of me and I related the product to a personal experience. Then I shared my affiliate link.

What would have made even more of an impact is if I had a picture of me with the actual charger in my hand. I even tagged Seven Springs Ski Resort just in case they see the post and share it with others who are in any way affiliated with Seven Springs as owners, employees or guests (growing my audience). Overall, however, I tried to catch the attention of my audience not only with pictures but also with a few short sentences as well. Just FYI - I sold around 20 of these little $20 devices in about 10 minutes.

A quick note- in some instances, you will need to or may want to at least purchase the products or try the services you're reselling. Personnel testimonials from the seller are #1.

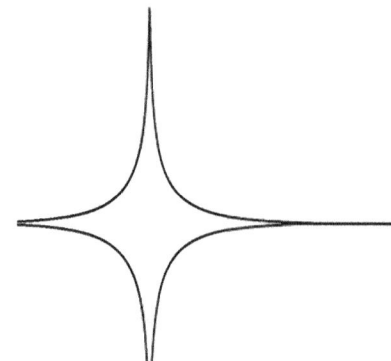

Getting People to Share – Sharing is caring, as they say. If you have a social media following, this makes posting and selling much easier and also makes sharing more probable. But what makes sharing a post most probable is the content of the post. For my Facebook post above, there is a low probability that anyone would share that. Why? It's not engaging enough. Videos get more Shares than any other type of post. According to Wave.com, "Videos get 1200% more shares than text and images combined. That's because they have the power to evoke strong emotions that encourage viewers to comment, like, and share. The better the content, the more interaction it receives."

That said, if this was a more in depth video of the product while I was skiing, the post may have been more engaging and therefore more likely to be shared. If I made it funny by falling while skiing and still show the device in good working condition, the engagement and share level would have gone through the roof. You get the point. In summary, the best content is quality video-based content that gets shared. In addition, whichever platform you choose, create content that gets shared.

PROMOTE YOUR BUSINESS

As I stated at the very beginning of this book in the Disclaimer, everything in this book can be found online. These days, you can search Google for just about anything. What I have done is conducted the hours and hours of searching and reading and listening to gather the information into one convenient, low cost compilation so everything is right in front of you. The reason this book is priced so low is because I chose not to rip people off by providing information that can be found online for free. This is what a lot of people do (and I found so very many in all of my research!) They offer you courses, eBooks, books, and other highly priced systems, courses or seminars where they upsell a bunch of other crap that you probably don't need. The point is that when it comes to how to promote or market your product or services, everyone has a different strategy and that doesn't mean that your strategy is wrong or right.

Marketing 101 - Research shows that customers who get a tailored, curated experience are more likely to make a purchase. Ask the question - how can you deliver a more personalized customer experience? First of all, and again, know our audience. In most cases, as mentioned above, short-form and quick video content is the key. This type of content now dominates social media. TikTok and Instagram reels and even YouTube Shorts are now the place for brand content. Younger audiences have traditionally been the prime target with these reels, but data shows older demographics are quickly catching up by starting to watch and share reels and shorts as well.

Choose which platform where your target audience is most likely to engage on social media. TikTok attracts a younger audience with the majority of its users between ages 13-34. However, there has been an increase in people over the age of 45 using TikTok. Instagram has a more diverse audience, with nearly half of all users falling between the ages of 18 and 34 but a strong user base in ages 35-60. Facebook's highest amount of users are between the ages of 18-54. YouTube Shorts is another platform that can likely resonate with a target audience of people of all ages.

Connection in marketing means so much for our business, your brand and sells. Connecting with your customers and clients and those who follow you on social media is huge. This can happen in several ways. You can interact with your followers when they leave comments. You can follow up with a customer after a sell or after they have used your services. You can also develop an email list and follow up with customers in this manner or periodically provide them with useful information about your products or your industry in general.

Again because there are so many different types of marketing now, it's a good idea to do your research to understand what will work best for your particular products, services and audience. Here are some examples you can utilize:

- Social media marketing (e.g. posts, paid advertisements)
- Mobile marketing (e.g. texts, push notifications based on users' location or interest/behaviors on internet searches, social media and website visits)
- Email marketing (e.g. newsletters, links to your website)
- Content marketing (e.g. social media posts, newsletters, podcasts)
- Affiliate marketing (e.g. hiring someone to sell your products/services)
- Influencer marketing (e.g. teaming with influencers to promote your products/services)
- Telemarketing (e.g. paid services to reach potential customers)
- Direct marketing (e.g. in this instance, selling your own products/services)
- Search engine marketing (e.g. paying to increase visibility to website/online presence)

Build a Website – Nowadays, you can build your shop/store right on your social media store/page. There are some very simple platforms that exist where you can build a very simple website. If you build one yourself, get someone to help or pay for someone to build one for you and connect your social media platforms to it. ON EVERY PAGE. In other words, send users to your website for the purchase of products and services. When marketing products and services it's always good to have a website that people can come to, not only to purchase your products and services but so they can learn more about you and your business.

Clients and customers feel more comfortable sharing your products and services and becoming repeat customers when they see legitimacy to your business. I talk about how to build a website for free or for very little a month (quite often less than $20 a month) later in this book. You can have a robust, mobile friendly website or app (if you don't' already have one) without knowing how to write any code.

The best part about sending people to your website is you can collect their data (email, phone, social media) and build a brand-to-customer relationship with that individual right on your own platform. This can also be done with online surveys and other data collection methods.

Overall, with new laws changing the way cookies and tracking are now being utilized, keep your marketing efforts on the forward thinking methodology toward the future. This will keep you ahead of the game on all levels. This also benefits when you are creating a promotion and marketing budget.

Budgeting to Promote - With all the new terminology being pushed around the marketing circle, there are still free methods of marketing that work. As mentioned earlier, there are two types of budgetary marketing strategies:

- Organic or Grassroots
- Paid

In this book I will use the term "grassroots" which refers to any type of marketing strategy that you don't have to pay for. Here are a few:

- Creating shareable content
- Joining Facebook or other social media groups that allow you to solicit
- Asking for referrals
- Partnering with other influencers
- Attending free networking or business events
- Cold calling

Although there are other grassroots marketing strategies, one of the best grassroots strategies to market is to create content that people will like and share. As mentioned in the section on **Building A Following**, you can organically market products and services by creating sharable content. This is ultimately the best solution and causes memes, videos, reels, etc. to go viral.

Join Facebook or other social media groups related to your services or products. These groups can pose many benefits and also increase your following. Some Facebook groups are private groups and have rules to which you must agree in order to join. Sometimes the rules include no soliciting within the group. But there are also groups that let you promote or solicit. Be mindful that the groups that allow you to solicit may have hundreds if not thousands of others doing the exact same thing. This is where you get creative in your posts (e.g. videos that capture). Try creating your own group and inviting people you believe would have an interest in your product or services. Ask others to refer you to customers and promote your product or service to others that may have an interest.

Partnering with influencers can be extremely beneficial. For example, when I was building one of my online businesses, Dormoney.com, I researched social media influencers that have a decent following of around 10K. I figured that these influencers had to have some relevancy to my business model. I did not want to target influencers with larger followings for several reasons that I discuss later in the **Section 11 Influencer**.

Television – Many people don't know that you can buy local cable or TV commercial spots for as little as $2 per commercial spot on some major networks like History channel, CNN, MSN and others. For example, Comcast, Verizon, Cox and other local cable companies have both digital (online) and TV based advertising. Many of these TV networks range in cost. For example, to get on CNN it may cost between $10 - $20 per 30 second commercial spot vs. TNT for $7 per commercial spot. The digital component is mainly online adverting across the cable company's reach.

The TV side of marketing will be based on the local area in which you are targeting. On the flip side, with so many people now moving away from cable, streaming sites like Hulu and others also offer low-cost adverting starting at $500 for local TV stations. Because TV commercials as well as any form of advertisement are based on the frequency of how often the viewer sees it or impressions, the more you run the commercial, the better the response. Also note that you will have costs for shooting your commercial if you do not know how to do that yourself.

- Suggested Budget - $3000 - $7000 (on the low end)
- Term – 6 to 9 months

Radio – Radio ads can be very expensive. It greatly depends on the station. The recommended budget includes both satellite radio as well as your local radio stations. Again, because each station has its own demographics and each station typically caters to a specific type of audience, choose the station that best fits your target audience. Most listeners to both local and satellite radio stations are mainly listing during peak hours, typically during morning and afternoon rush hour commutes. There is an audience of online listeners of radio stations also. Check with your local station for the demographical information about these listeners.

- Suggested Budget - $3000 - $7000
- Term – 6 to 9 months

Social Media Ads – As nearly the entire world (upwards of 75% of the world's almost 8 billion people) is on some form of social media platform, you cannot go wrong with ads on these outlets. Each one has a ton of settings from which you can choose that will help target your audience. These settings consider such demographics as users' interests, income, purchasing behaviors, lifestyles, careers, family status and more. Try to figure out which social media networks perform well organically for your brand, products or services.

Each platform can have a different objective for your audience. For example, Instagram and Facebook ads appear in user feeds, stories, marketplace and other areas of the platform. There are also different types of ads that you can create such as image ads, carousel, video, collection, slideshow, stories, etc. On Instagram and Facebook, you can "boost" posts, create ad reels or even advertise your Instagram or Facebook shop. Other social media platforms such as YouTube, TikTok, Twitter, LinkedIn, Snapchat, Pinterest, and others all have different audience settings when targeting and creating your ads.

Here are the two most important components for marketing on social media (connecting knowledge from **Build A Following** above):

- Create consistent quality content
- Create content that will be shared

A note of caution... please don't spend all of your money with only one platform. Spread out your budget across different platforms. Start with a minimal amount (as low as $30 even) and then slowly increase the budget for each add after you receive good results from measuring your insights. You will be able to see the analytics of your ads and how they performed from your backend ad account on these platforms. Therefore, create multiple ads, test them, look at how the ads performed, correct them if necessary, then promote the ads that worked.

- Suggested Budget - $300 - $3000
- Term – 6 to 9 months

Your budget greatly depends on several factors such as your risk tolerance and amount of expendable capital. Marketing is considered the life blood of a business along with customer service management (CSM). Figure 2 below takes into account someone that is an employee, makes a decent salary and still has bills to pay. The below offers a suggested amount of how much you should put aside each week to build up funds for your marketing budget. Remember, invest in yourself.

Annual Salary	30K	40K	50K	60K	70K	80K	90K	100K
Suggested amount to invest/spend weekly for marketing.	$25	$50	$75	$100	$110	$125	$135	$150

Figure 2

That may seem like a lot, especially when you already have bills to pay. However, if you consider your marketing and investing budget as you do your other bills, it will benefit you in both the short and the long run. (Connecting knowledge from the *Saving Money* section.)

You are using your marketing money to build your business. Using the $50K salary as an example, at $75 per week, your available marketing budget would be $300 per month. This $300 to spend on ads on social media over one month, with the quality shareable content, you could double that $300. That means, reimbursing your marketing budget the $300 you spent and profiting an additional $300. Make marketing and investing one of your normal bills if you are going to run your business successfully.

PROTECT YOU AND YOUR BUSINESS

For so many reasons such as liability, taxes and personal peace of mind, I strongly, highly and earnestly admonish you to create your business structure and do it properly. This is done through your state agency business filing entity (usually the Secretary of State but check your state for the proper agency). There are several business structures to choose from, for example, C corporation, S corporation (a tax status choice), LLC, partnerships, etc.

I always suggest corporations over LLCs. Why? Because the IRS can disregard that an LLC entity is technically separate and distinct from the owner. Essentially, this means that you typically file the LLC business tax information with your personal tax returns through Schedule C. Therefore, taxes will flow through your personal tax return and you will be personally liable for the income and your tax status from there. If you create an LLC, elect with the IRS to be taxed as a corporation. The default is to be treated as a C-Corporation. In this case, the IRS will treat your business as a separate taxpayer. As a result, the business reports all income and deductions on IRS Form 1120 each year and pays the corresponding income tax. But if that's the tax election you're going to choose, you might as well create a Corporation.

There's so much hype surrounding the creation of your business... and those that want you to pay them hundreds, even thousands of dollars to do it for you. There are so many companies offering paid "quick business creation services". If you do not know exactly what business structure will work best for you and your industry, do your research. A great place to start is your state agency. Study the information offered on your state's website. You cannot go wrong here. If you have any questions, I highly suggest reaching out to the state agency where you have to file your business. They have all the answers. No, they cannot give you advice particular to your situation but they can certainly give you the correct information so that you can make good decisions. If, after all of your research, you still feel it is necessary to seek a professional, by all means please do so. A business consultant, tax professional or attorney can certainly help you make the best decision based on your personal and particular needs and what will work best for you and your business.

PAY YOUR TAXES

People get in trouble with tax issues because they do not file their state or federal taxes or they try to evade taxes without knowing how to legally avoid paying taxes on their money. The penalties for not filing and not paying taxes range from fines, including interest, to jail time. Many times people end up owing tens of thousands of dollars because they get audited after filing taxes but subsequently cannot produce the receipts for their business expenses claimed on those tax returns. Don't get caught up in this trap. I highly recommend that you talk to a tax professional and remember these tips when trying navigate the tax law:

- Don't mix your personal taxes with your business taxes.
- Do your research.
- Be a good planner.
- Open up a corporation versus an LLC (but by all means establish your business entity in some manner with your appropriate state agency and remain in good standing).
- Keep all of your receipts.
- Know what you can legally deduct and what you cannot.
- Report your profits and losses honestly.
- PAY YOUR TAXES!

Don't mix your personal taxes with business taxes. Keep them separate. So many people try to lower their adjusted gross income (AGI) with a bunch of (Schedule C) business deductions and find themselves getting away with it or a few years or so and then POW! – you get hit right in the kisser with that IRS letter that asked you for your receipts from three years ago and the receipts are faded or crumbled up pieces of paper. Not getting accepted.

Consult a tax professional. There is so much information out there for free that will guide you on what can be legally done to lower your tax obligation through business related tax solutions and best practices. This is all being done every day, every year by the rich and wealthy and guess what? It is all legal and legit. The tax code is extremely complicated but it is extremely friendly to the wealthy.

Be good planner. Being successful at business means that you can plan ahead well. This book will show how to make money online upwards of $10K+ a month. Don't get so consumed with profit and money that you forget to pay your taxes on that money. Plan ahead and establish a dedicated account specifically for paying taxes.

Many suggest keeping your receipts from the last three years and that is primarily due to the fact that you have three years to file your Federal taxes (e.g. you have until 2025 to file your 2022 taxes). However, I suggest keeping all of your receipts for at least 10 years. Some states can go back further than 10 years with an audit of your business taxes. Make sure you keep your receipts in both electronic form and paper form. This covers you if either one goes missing.

So many people get in trouble with the IRS because they are trying to deduct expenses through their personal tax returns that the IRS only allows a percentage for. For example, you can't deduct your entire mortgage if you're using only 25% of your home for your business. You can deduct the interest but not the mortgage. Please do thorough research on tax deductions for businesses.

BUILDING YOUR BUSINESS SYSTEM

A lot people have come up to me and have asked, "what's the secret to a successful business" or they ask me "how can I get rich quick, the legal way and without running a scam". I always answer this way- "You can get rich quick, legally without scamming people as well and that's real, and it's about what you do with the money once you get it quickly. But the best way to maintain wealth is to create a business that sells itself."

Let's jump a little into this. Remember earlier I said to you "don't chase money"? Stop chasing money. If you chase money, it will run from you, literally. The key to earning lots of money and on a consistent basis is to build a system where the money comes to you. You do this by solving a problem or need. If you create a business that solves a problem or need, people will literally throw money at you. If you honestly engaged in enough conversations with individuals and start asking questions about the challenges they're facing, they will tell you what they think is actually needed to help solve a problem. They will tell you what business to start without even actually saying, "hey, start this business". There are opportunities in everything we do, hear, speak and see. The key is to figure out how you can build a system that delivers this need to others. Here are some important questions to ask yourself.

- What do people need and want and would easily buy from me if I had it?
- How much will it cost me to produce?
- Who already has it and if no one does, how can I get it built?
- How many people are trying this already?
- How well does my solution fit within society?
- What is the difference before versus after they buy my solution?
- What is the difference between my solution and the competition?

You can earn a decent income from any of the options in this book. But the question is, in essence, how can you take from this book and build a business in such a way that people come to you to buy your service or product? How can you ensure that you're no longer chasing the money? Keep in mind that it's all about identifying problems or gaps with existing products or services. You can come up with new ideas. However, new ideas without having large amounts of capital are tough to come by, or at least good ones. But problems? They are everywhere! Almost every product or service you use on a daily basis was created to solve a problem.

When it comes to solving problems, there are two main types- original fix and enhancement. The Original Fix is needing to get the chicken from one side of a road to another. So the answer (or the idea) is to build a mode a transportation that will take the chicken there. However, if transportation already existed, but the issue was that it took a full day to cross the road, you could come up with the idea to speed that process by adding an engine that you create. This is an Enhancement. The enhancement option is generally easier, and quite often many new ideas, products and services are developed from something that already existed. I can go on and on about how to build a system. Ultimately, the choice is up to you and how you develop the best way for money to come to you so that you don't have to chase money.

MINDSET

What you think and how you think about money matters...

When you are unemployed or jobless, don't have any capital to start or even any incoming monies, to earn additional income Mindset is everything. What does that mean? When broke, quite often people tell themselves indirectly or speak indirect affirmations to themselves. Let's use Joe as an example. Joe just lost his job at Home Depot due to budget cuts. He was making a decent enough salary to at least maintain a small 1-bedroom apartment in a low-income neighborhood. In transition from being unemployed, he now collects unemployment and has been on several interviews looking for another job. Recently a family member in need asks Joe for some money. Here's how Joe responded. These are statements or affirmations that many people make when someone asks them for money, and they do not have very much to give:

1. I'm running a little low on funds.
2. I'm feeling the pinch at the moment.
3. I'm temporarily in the red.
4. I'm nearly running on empty.
5. My resources are a little depleted.
6. My bank balance is a little bit strained.
7. My finances are a little strained at the moment.
8. I'm a little cleaned out at the moment.
9. I don't have any money now.
10. I need money now and I don't have a job.
11. I'm broke.
12. I don't have any money.
13. I don't have it right now.
14. Let me check to see what I have (although they know already).
15. Right now, money is tight.

Should I go on? I am pretty sure you get the point.

Just look at the above statements people tell themselves, including Joe. Off course he is broke. He just affirmed this in 15 different ways. You may have also spoken one of these statements to yourself or another person as well. That is mindset.

Let us say these affirmations differently:

1. Ok. Let's figure out how to get that amount. Let's pool our resources, work together and accomplish this goal.
2. I know how we can get it; let's go to work here and do this.
3. I have a way you can get this amount. Listen to my solutions and let's work together to get the amount we need.

What you think of money and how you think of money is important. In the evolving global landscape, the traditional 9-to-5 job is no longer the only way to earn a substantial income. You must have multiple sources of income. For example, let's look at some:

1. Job
2. "Side Hustle" – Cleaning houses, landscaping, etc.
3. Monthly dividend stocks
4. Rental property
5. And about 30 more online sources....

However, in this book, I only cover about 10 and from this book you'll learn that there are so many sources of income that you can generate. Many individuals now earn money through entrepreneurial ventures, freelancing, investments, and other non-traditional means. Amid these varying paths to wealth, one constant remains: the power of mindset. Having the right mindset is arguably the most critical facet to earning large amounts of money without having a conventional job or while you are working your regular 9 to 5. Here's why:

Visionary Thinking – The non-traditional routes to wealth often require one to think outside the box. When you are not tied to a set job with a fixed income, your earnings potential is bound only by your imagination and drive. People with a growth mindset envision opportunities where others see challenges. They transform ideas into profitable ventures, which is quintessential in arenas like startup culture, real estate investments, and online businesses.

Don't get me wrong. I'm all about multiple sources of income and I do believe in side-hustles. However, quite a few of them are either confined to the local area, temporary or not scalable. I'm going to show you how to build an online "Business System" - which is a business model or system of automated processes you create that:

1. Solve problems
2. Spend less time managing
3. Have great customer service
4. Spend less capital to market the business
5. Are Scalable
6. Market themselves
7. Attract money

Risk Tolerance - Engaging in endeavors outside the conventional employment structure often involves higher risk. However, the rewards can be tremendous. A resilient mindset equips individuals with the courage to take calculated risks and the perseverance to keep going even when faced with setbacks. There's a quote that I live by and that is:

"Focus and fail fast. Learn quickly and try something new. If you can focus, you can succeed" – Bill Gates

Whereas those with a fixed mindset may retreat at the first sign of trouble, those with a robust, adaptive mindset see failures as learning opportunities. In other words, you will be taking a risk.

Self-Motivation and Discipline – Probably the most important components of the millionaire mindset. Without the structured environment of a traditional job, it becomes essential to self-motivate. Procrastination can be your biggest enemy when you are your own boss or when you are navigating the volatile world of investments. A strong mindset ensures that you set goals, stick to them, and remain disciplined in your approach, allowing for consistent growth and wealth accumulation.

Again, you must focus and become obsessed with succeeding.

Learning and Adaptability - The world of non-traditional income is ever-changing New technologies, market fluctuations, and evolving consumer behaviors can turn today's profitable venture into tomorrow's outdated model. A proactive mindset, centered on continuous learning and adaptability, ensures you stay ahead of the curve, capitalizing on new opportunities and pivoting when necessary.

If you take my course at ReprogramMyMind.com I talk about:

Relationship Building, Mastermind Team and Networking - Wealth is not just about individual effort. You must have a team... or at least let me say that it's best to have a team or partner with whom you are building wealth. Your team must be able to follow your vision, or you follow the team's vision collectively. It's always better to build wealth with a team of people or one other person. The more people around you that are wealthy or that help you get wealthy, will naturally increase your wealth.

Building with friends and family first is always my initial thought. However, not all your friends or all your family members will support you or motivate you with your dreams or goals. Those that do are the ones that you need on your team. Quite often your friends and family will be the most loyal, understand you personally and will motivate you to continue no matter the adversity. This can be your mastermind team.

Relationship building is all about your network. Building or developing a strong network is essential to success. When you need people or people with resources, you need to be able to make a quick call and get things done on time and the right way. Having a vast, loyal and trustworthy network is important. A positive and open mindset can make you more approachable, trustworthy, and collaborative- traits that are invaluable in these settings.

Financial Awareness and Intelligence – Earning money is just one part of the equation. In this book, I'll teach you how, instead of chasing money, you build a business system that is automated, and money will be attracted to you. In other words, if you follow the procedures in the book, you'll be able to earn money while you sleep and start your own automated business system. I teach more about business systems in my courses online at ReprogramMyMind.com.

Keeping money and growing money is other part of the equation. This requires financial intelligence, which is not just about understanding numbers but also about cultivating a mindset that prioritizes long-term gains over short-term pleasures. Those with a solid mindset can discern between good and bad investments, save diligently, and make money work for them through avenues like stocks, real estate, business systems or even passive income streams online as well as invest in other people's businesses, startups, etc.

Don't Underprice or Overprice your Products or Services – Know what you're worth and it better not be pennies. You are worth way more than a few dollars. I don't even know you and I can tell you that your life is worth more than gold.

Here's an important question- Is your service and product the same? Many entrepreneurs often grapple with pricing their services or products. Underpricing can limit your earning potential, while overpricing can alienate potential clients. There is also a type of pricing called "High Ticket" product or service. A confident mindset allows you to recognize your worth, ensuring that you don't undervalue your offerings.

While skills, networks, and opportunities play crucial roles in earning substantial money outside of traditional jobs, it's the mindset that acts as the foundation. A mindset anchored in vision, resilience, adaptability, and belief in oneself can unlock doors to unlimited wealth potential. As the saying goes:

"It's not your aptitude, but your attitude, that determines your altitude."

And when it comes to financial success without a conventional job, this couldn't be truer. Strong focus, the power of intention and a positive mental attitude is key to being able to attract money.

Why "Attracting Money" is Important – Money, despite its tangible and numerical nature, carries with it an emotional and psychological weight. While many individuals approach their finances from a scarcity mindset, which revolves around fear and limitation, a more empowering approach is adopting an "attract-money" perspective. This perspective is rooted in the belief that money is not just a finite resource, but something you can actively attract more of into your life through various means. I'm not going to dive into any biblical references to understanding why our Creator designed up to be prosperous and creators ourselves, but understanding the importance of this viewpoint can revolutionize how we relate to money and subsequently, how we manage, accumulate and attract wealth.

Cultivating a Positive Relationship with Money – My students always ask me "how" to do this. The answer may sound simple. However, with anything you want to master, you must first practice, study, practice more and then thrive for mastery. This goes for your mind as well. If you want to change your mindset about money, you must develop then practice the money mindset to master it.

When we view money from a place of abundance rather than shortage, we begin to foster a healthier, more positive relationship with it. Many people carry negative associations or beliefs about money from past experiences, family history, low vibrational friends and family, school, social media algorithms (be careful what you scroll your attention on) or societal teachings. These negative beliefs can hinder our ability to earn, save, and invest effectively. By adopting an attract-money perspective, you start to see money as a tool that can be leveraged, rather than a stressor to be feared or even something you must chase. We'll get into understanding how not to chase money in subsequent chapters.

The Power of Visualization – One of the cornerstones of the attract-money perspective is the power of visualization. This is so important, and we must have focus.

"Focus is the superpower to success."

When we focus our mental energies on the wealth we want to achieve, we subconsciously start aligning our actions with that vision. This is so very true. There are many case studies that have validated the power of visualization in achieving goals, be it in sports, academics, or finances. Visualizing success can pave the way for tangible steps to realize that success. I always recommend writing things down and revisiting written work daily and making any changes.

Taking Action – You must take action. You can't just sit around on your back side and think that the money will fall in your lap. It doesn't work that way. The attract - money mindset is not just about wishful thinking; it's about taking active steps towards your financial goals. When we believe that we can attract money, we are more inclined to educate ourselves on financial matters, seek out investment opportunities, or even embark on entrepreneurial ventures. This proactive attitude propels us forward, turning dreams into actionable plans thereby bringing what we desire into our reality.

Be Ready for Opportunities - Those who believe in attracting money are more receptive to new opportunities. Whether it's a new job offer, an investment tip, or a business partnership, they are more likely to recognize and seize these opportunities because they're attuned to them. In contrast, a scarcity mindset might lead one to overlook or even mistrust such opportunities, out of fear or skepticism. This is why you must be in tunned to self, becoming aware of who you are, what's really being presented to you and of course, "do your research.

Facilitating Resilience – You must be resilient, passionate and obsessed with succeeding. Trust me and understand that you will fail. Fail fast, learn, get your butt back up and keep going. Financial journeys are rarely straightforward. There will be setbacks – bad investments, business losses, or unexpected expenses. However, when one is rooted in the attract-money mindset, they see these setbacks not as definitive failures but as learning experiences, confident in their ability to attract more wealth in the future.

Be Generous - When we view money from an abundance mindset, we are less likely to hoard and more likely to give. This doesn't only benefit the recipients of our generosity but us as well. Numerous studies have shown that giving, whether in terms of charitable donations or personal gifts, enhances our own sense of happiness and well-being.

Create Your Legacy and Build Your Generational Wealth - the attractmoney perspective isn't just about personal accumulation. Those who truly believe in the power to attract wealth often have bigger visions – be it for their families, communities, or causes of which they are passionate. They're not just amassing wealth but creating legacies.

In essence, viewing money from an "attract-money" perspective goes beyond mere financial mechanics. It's a holistic approach that combines mindset, emotion, and action. It not only reshapes our individual financial destinies but can also inspire and uplift those around us, creating a ripple effect of prosperity and positive change.

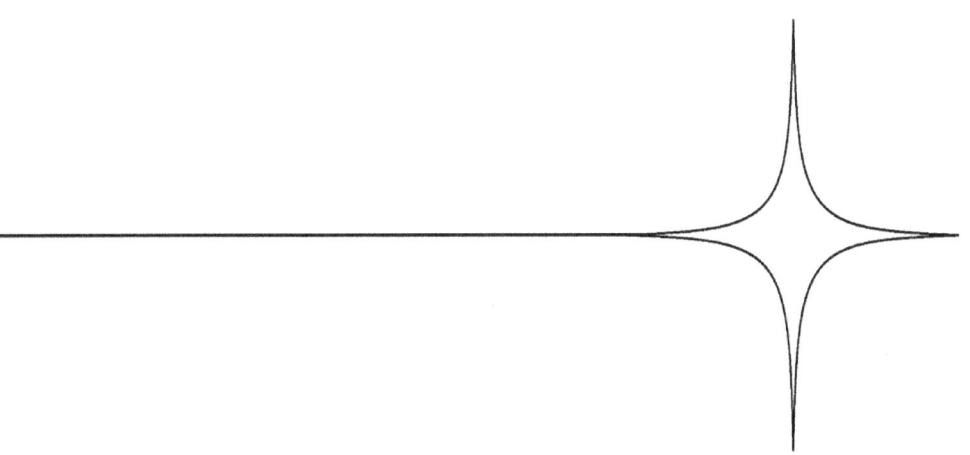

PART 2

HOW TO EARN
INCOME ONLINE

SECTION 1
AFFILIATE MARKETING
(FREELANCE DIGITAL MARKETING)

QUALIFYING FACTORS	GRADE
Difficulty Level (DL)	2.5
Realistic Earning Potential (REP)	$1 - $1000 Per Day
Monetary Investment (MI)	Minimal
Potential Time Commitment (PTC)	1 - 4 hr/day
Suggested Marketing Structure (SMS)	Grassroots, Paid or Both

Affiliate Marketing (AM) is when you earn a commission by promoting a product or service made by another retailer or business using an affiliate link. It is an online practice of joining specific websites that house a list of businesses and copying "affiliate" links and then promoting them through a series of either social media profile pages, websites/blogs or even text messages and other word of mouth processes. Some AM programs can reward you for leads, free trials, clicks to a website, or getting downloads of a mobile app. Most affiliate marketing programs are free to join so that does away with any start up fees. If done right, (if you have a solid following combined with paid ads on social media) you can earn up to $1000 a day or more.

Below is a list of some of the most used companies on the web that will allow you to open free accounts and start copying links, sharing these links and generating income.

Pros and Cons

Pros

Affiliate Marketing works and it works very well. If you're good at selling, utilizing online resources and social media, you can easily earn up to $2K - $5K per month, especially if you already have the forum or following via social media. Shareable content is the key word when using grassroots methods to promote your affiliate links.

Most affiliate links are free so quite often there are no startup costs. Investing small amounts of capital into effective paid ads equips you to start generating profits faster. Another pro tip to using AM, is that yes, you can quite often sit back and not worry about shipping, taxes or in some cases promotion. This is because many of the companies selling these products or services do quite a bit a marketing. Choose wisely on which products/services you promote. Affiliates get access to thousands of products across several marketplaces, making finding the right product to promote for target audiences simple, easy and based on your personal preferences.

There are tons of affiliate marketing programs that will allow you as the affiliate to choose products in the niches that interest you the most. You can also choose to become a part of affiliate programs that offer high commissions. You don't have to settle for promoting products that you don't think will earn you much money.

Cons

There are some downsides to AM. You have to have a following or create one because you have to have customers. Also, it will help tremendously if you invest in advertising. Another downside is that, unless you have actually tried some of the products and services yourself, you may be promoting a scam, a dangerous service or product with very low quality customer satisfaction, even if that product or service had lots of great reviews. It is possible that the company paid people to write those positive reviews. It is highly recommended that you conduct heavy research into any product you are going to promote through AM.

As an affiliate marketer you lack control over a product's or service's quality, customer support, and branding. Most times, the money from the sale goes to the merchant, and affiliates only get paid after the purchase is fully processed.

Realism – Don't let the YouTube, TikTok and Instagram reels and shorts fool you into thinking that it's super easy to make money online through affiliate marketing. There are so many influencers already doing some sort of AM that you can quite often fall in the mix of the thousands if you don't structure good marketing strategies. Many of these online "let me show you how I made $5000 in one month" social media posters make that big money with AM because they have a ton of subscribers or followers, so the influence is already there for them to make sells. If you don't have some sort of following, subscribers, web traffic, etc., be prepared to work or invest money to grow your audience or promote your product or service using AM.

1.	Amazon Affiliate Program and Amazon Associate Program	affiliate-program.amazon.com	The Programs are very similar. As an Affiliate, you get a unique link to post and earn a commission when someone orders that specific product from your link. You must make at least one sale within 180 days of signing up or your account will be shut down. As an Associate, if someone clicks on your personalized link, you earn a commission. If someone buys that product using your link, you earn an additional commission. Further, if someone uses that link but then goes on to buy another product, you earn a commission on that also. If your following and sales meet the qualifying threshold, you could additionally become a part of the Amazon Influencer Program.
2.	Udemy	udemy.com/affiliate	A ton of online courses from website design to mobile app design, adobe products, video editing courses and so much more. As an Affiliate you will drive your followers to the site via your link. When they purchase the course, you receive a commission.

3.	Ebay Partner Network	partnernetwork.eba y.com	More than just used items. Quite often new items are sold are Ebay. As an Affiliate you will drive people to your products on Ebay's website and you will get a commission from each purchase.
4.	Rakuten	rakutenadvertising com/affiliate/	Rakuten is a global advertising company that can connect you to affiliate marking for a multitude of products and services. These connections include physical and digital offers from big brands like Lego, Nvidia, Microsoft, Lyft, Macy's, and JetBlue, for example.
5.	ShareASale	shareasale.com/inf o/	ShareASale focuses more on traditional physical offers. However you will find plenty of digital products on their platform, specifically software products.
6.	Market Health	markethealth.com/ affiliate.php	Aimed squarely at the health and beauty market. MarketHealth boasts that they are the highest paying affiliate program and has the best tracking software in their industry.
7.	SkillShare	skillshare.com/affili ates	SkillShare is similar to Udemy. As an Affiliate, at least one of your social media pages must be aligned with the company's brand. You earn a commission on every account that is created through your link.
8.	Avangate	avangatenetwork.c om/publishers/	Focuses on software products. Your social media page should align with their content. Avangate is often completely overlooked by affiliates who are too busy chasing offers on the bigger networks. This means you have a much better chance of finding untapped opportunities there.
9.	Clickbank	clickbank.com/affli ates/	Choose from a wide variety of categories with good payouts. Clickbank promises its product offerings are high quality and that they vet their products through federal compliance approvals to ensure you are selling top of the line products.
10.	Digistore24	digistore24.com/e n/home/affiliates	Mainly digital products in a wide variety of areas such as health, sports, home and garden, personal development and more.

SECTION 2
YOUR BRAND USING ALIBABA

QUALIFYING FACTORS	GRADE
Difficulty Level (DL)	3
Realistic Earning Potential (REP)	$1 - $5000 Per Month
Monetary Investment (MI)	High
Potential Time Commitment (PTC)	4 - 8 hr/per/day
Suggested Marketing Structure (SMS)	Paid

Alibaba is China's biggest online commerce company which is publicly traded in the United States. Alibaba also owns two other sites, Taobao and Tmall. Alibaba, Taobao and Small have low cost, quality products from made in China. Why there is some controversy surrounding China's labor rights, these sites have hundreds of millions of users, and hosts numerous merchants and businesses. Alibaba handles more business than any other e-commerce company.

But how can you earn money? Answer – 2 ways:

- Order products mainly in bulk with a minimal purchase order (MPO) - meaning you have to purchase a certain number of units for example, 100, and then resell them through another e-commerce site like Amazon, Esty, Facebook Marketplace, OfferUp or some other very well known market place where consumers come to purchase items.

- Order products mainly in bulk with a MPO and then resell them on **your own** e-commerce site.

In both instances, you will have to handle shipping (unless you have your customers assume this charge) and also in both instances, you can have the products customized with your company name, logo, etc., basically your brand where you are creating your own merchandise.

In *Section 11 Influencer*, I explain how you can use your social media posts to brand, sell and market your business. This can also go in direct correlation to buying and selling products directly from Alibaba. And if you want to sell your own brand of merchandise through these same platforms, most vendors on Alibaba will customize your items which can then in turn be resold for a greater return.

For example, I personally sell sports products through Alibaba, e.g., basketball sleeves. I purchase at minimal at least 100 pairs at $4 per pair = $400 plus shipping $100 (from China) for a total of $500. These basketball sleeves of course have my company logo, branding on the tag and my design and colors. I then resell them on my website (after promotion on social media) and through social media for $10.

- Total Spent $500
- Total Earned $1000
- **Total Profit $500**

Pros and Cons

Pros

You can build your own brand with Alibaba. Most people customize the products that they purchase from Alibaba with their own business logo. You can put as much time into the business as you'd like. This is what makes selling through Alibaba very scalable. Additionally, there are several different business models and pricing tiers you can implement that will allow you to reach all types of customers. The income potential is very high if you can market and deliver a quality product that people want. In addition, you can utilize other methods for delivery of your products such as:

- Amazon FBA
- Dropshipping
- Other methods

Quite often what the successful resellers do is find products that are selling well on other websites. For example, I sell a high performance sports mouth guard from Alibaba to youth sports organizations across my local area. I purchased the mouth piece for around $4 (does not include shipping from China to the U.S.) and resold them for $15. I had my company brand placed on the mouth guard and the packaging.

Cons

Depending on what you purchase, your influence, storage and other circumstances, selling through Alibaba can be expensive mainly because you essentially have to buy the products, pay for shipping (and in some cases, there can be shipping delays), promote and market products.

As you learned above, you can do grassroots or paid advertising. Competition is also high on Alibaba, so it's important that you research the market and understand where the demand lies for each product that you're trying to sell. There is no safety net. These products are coming from overseas. You can order samples to determine the quality of the product (samples will cost) and if you want to proceed with a bulk order based on the quality of the samples, you can do that.

Ordering samples is also a good way to test your product with a few customers to determine, again, if you want to proceed with a bulk order. Overall, you will be spending money on inventory that you pay for up front before selling (and hopefully selling out) in order to earn a profit.

Alibaba, and by default AliExpress was primarily discussed here because quite frankly, they are the tops for cost effectiveness and potential for earning extremely high profits selling your own branded merchandise. However, here are a few other e-commerce websites worth an Honorable Mention.

	NAME	WEBSITE	INFORMATION
1.	Global Sources	globalsources.com	Likely Alibaba's biggest competitor. It is a bit tougher for manufacturers to sell on Global Sources because their requirements in the industry are stricter. This could be a plus for products in terms of quality but some items may be pricier.
2.	Deluxe	deluxe.com/products/	Large inventory to create custom items. Prices may prove much higher and less negotiable than Global Sources and Alibaba.
3.	Wholesale Central	wholesalecentral.com/index.htm	Products include office like supplies and this makes sense as the company is owned by Staples.

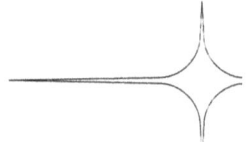

44

SECTION 3
ARTIFICIAL INTELLEGENCE

QUALIFYING FACTORS	GRADE
Difficulty Level	3.5
Realistic Earning Potential (REP)	$1 - $5000 Per Month
Monetary Investment (MI)	Medium
Potential Time Commitment (PTC)	4 - 6 hr/per/day
Suggested Marketing Structure (SMS)	Paid

Artificial Intelligence is the new wave of technology taking over our world as we know it. It's getting to the point that AI will become the new "employee" in the near future (and in some instances already has). Because AI is in a heightened form, you probably have seen the new AI apps that redo pictures of you or let you talk to an AI person like a companion. Even the video games are starting to utilize AI so the interaction with others is now in AI.

Stocks, crypto and other high level AI bots are being developed to build out the best investment platforms that deliver the highest profits. How you earn money with this model is ultimately how you utilize each service or if you decide to invest directly in an already existing company or start up. For example, there several AI websites/apps that you can use In relationship to freelancer websites like Upwork.com, Fiverr.com or Freelancer.com *(the subject of these types of sites are discussed in Section 7 Remote Work)*.

For example purposes only, let's say you created a profile as a social media post writer or blog post writer for $20 per post on one of the freelancer websites from above. Then you go to an AI site like Jasper.ai (lowest priced is $40 per month) to write the blog post or social media post and resell it to your freelancer client for a profit. If you're able to have the AI write 10 posts in a day for you at $20 a post then you just earned $200 in one day minus the monthly $40 website usage fee. That's $160 profit in one day (and your monthly fee is paid so your next $200 or more that month is just straight profit).

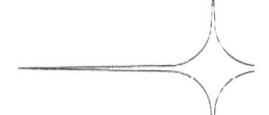

If you're able to do this across multiple freelancer sites, then of course you could profit very well. Please note that most of the AI sites/apps have a monthly or per content cost so you will have an initial expense to use the AI sites.

AI Strategies – Used in conjunction with other sites, apps, services or products, AI is fastly becoming the new stream of income. Below is a list of AI sites/apps to help you develop a strategy to add to your multiple income streams. Using a simple strategy like the one above, you can utilize multiple AI sites/apps in combination with other sites/apps that allow you to streamline your business services and grow profits. Often, influencers and other social media socialites use or resale AI sites/apps as part of their affiliate marketing because they offer residual or recurring income. I did not rank these suggestions like I did in other sections mainly because many of the AI sites all do something different and can be utilized in so many different ways.

	NAME	WEBSITE	INFORMATION
1.	Jasper.ai	jasper.ai	Uses AI to write social media post, blogs, ads and other content.
2.	Lovo.ai	lovo.ai	Personal and professional voice overs for use with your posts or website videos.
3.	Invideo.io	invideo.io	Create professional videos in a matter of minutes. The Site has over 5,000 templates from which to choose.
4.	Remove.bg	remove.bg	Removes background from 99% of all images so that you can add your own background to your images. Want to post about how great a trip to Paris could be but you took the picture in your kitchen? Try Remove.bg to enhance your post.
5.	Synthesia.io	synthesia.io	Uses AI to create training videos, marketing videos, how-to videos and more. You can create your videos from your plain text documents.
6.	ConversioBot	conversiobot.com	Uses an AI bot on your website for chats and other lead generation services.
7.	Craiyon.com	craiyon.com	Free AI that can take your text and create an image.

Again, it's best to use the AI sites and apps in combination with other services you do. Like in the two examples above, you can resell the AI services like I do or you can use them in combination with other services and products you provide. AI can enhance and even speed up your efficiency and effectiveness.

SECTION 4

MONTHLY DIVIDEND STOCKS
(PLUS A BRIEF ON CRYPTOCURRENCY)

QUALIFYING FACTORS	GRADE
Difficulty Level (DL)	2
Realistic Earning Potential (REP)	$1 - $500 Per Month
Monetary Investment (MI)	Medium
Potential Time Commitment (PTC)	1 hr/per/day
Suggested Marketing Structure (SMS)	None

I am not a licensed financial advisor and I am not going to share my stock portfolio or offer financial advice or even list which stocks to buy because that would be partly giving you advice. I'm only going to provide you with insight on how monthly dividend stocks can serve as another path of your income stream.

I used an example earlier in the book where I suggested to not use traditional banks and only open and put your money in these types of accounts:

- Brokerage accounts or accounts that allow you to buy and sell stocks, electronic funds transfers (EFTs), calls, puts, options, etc.
- Gives you a debit card from the brokerage account

You can get these types of accounts from Brokerage Firms like:

- E-Trade
- TD Ameritrade
- And Others... (Do your research on other firms)

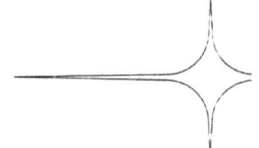

I will say this again- DO NOT PUT YOUR MONEY INTO TRADITIONAL BANKS - You will literally be throwing your money away. Let's again revisit the previous example on a more realistic level.

When you open up a Brokerage account, my suggestion is to immediately diversify and invest in stocks that payout monthly dividends. The dividend payment for a stock is stated on a per share basis and expressed by the dividends per share (DPS) ratio. This ratio is calculated by taking the total dividends paid out by a company over a period of time and dividing it by the total number of common stock shares held by its stockholders.

There are quite a few companies that pay monthly dividends and of course these monthly dividends can fluctuate depending on market conditions. Another way of viewing this is annual dividends are divided by 12 (months) and then paid out monthly.   For example, Company XYZ pays a $3 dividend annually, but distributes payouts monthly so if you divide that by 12 months, that's only .25 cents per share. That may seem like very little to earn every month.

However, if you have multiple shares of a stock that pay you .25 cents per share a month, that's good money.   Keep in mind that you still have to diversify. The question then becomes what stocks will pay me this amount? Below is a list of websites where you can find monthly dividend stocks. Please do your research and if necessary ask a licensed financial advisor. Some of these websites require you to have a membership to get full access to the list.

When you search a company to determine if you will invest in it, look at their dividend percentage to determine how to calculate the monthly payout. Some sites like Dividend.com will show you the monthly payout. For example, at the time of the writing of this book the company Realty Income Corp listed as "O" on the NYSE is going for $63.43 per share with an annual dividend percent yield of 4.70%. This computes to a $2.98 annual dividend and divided by 12 months = .24 cents paid per month. Using the sites below, research all of companies in which you would have an interest investing. Each company does something different and not all money is good money when it comes to investing in the stock market. Again, diversify your portfolio and don't let your money sit in regular banks.

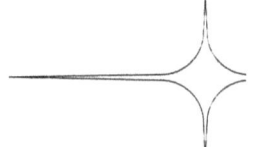

	NAME	WEBSITE	INFORMATION
1.	Dividend.com	dividend.com/monthly-income-from-monthly-dividend-stocks-etfs-and-funds/	One of the best sites for up to date performance information on stocks and monthly dividend payout calculations.
2.	DividendChannel.com	dividendchannel.com/monthly-dividend/	Provides a ranking of current monthly dividend yields by company. Also has on-topic articles about all things dividend stocks
3.	DividendDetective.com	dividenddetective.com/index.html	Dividend Detective, Harry Domash, provides tons of information including free resources on investing and dividend stocks. There is also an option to get a paid subscription to access even more information and access to the Dividend Detective.

A Brief on Cryptocurrency

Initially, when I starting writing this book, I was not going to include cryptocurrency as a topic to earn income online. Why? There are a vast number of crypto currencies that grow on a daily basis and some that have been going down for quite some time now but it can also be a fairly unstable investment choice.

The main reason I chose to include this section is the fact that the crypto industry has created wealth for many people and it continues to do so. The industry has had quite a few ups and downs (in fact some really low downs, for example Sam Bankman and FTX). Therefore, your personal research and study into the topic would be highly recommended before you jump full steam into crypto. I have personally seen my friends get wealthy off of crypto. But I've also seen some of my friends quit their jobs, take on the crypto trading full time and are now broke looking for another job only a few months later.

There are ultimately two ways to trade crypto.

- Through or with a legit trading platform like Forex, CoinBase, Binance, Crypto.com and many others; or
- There are several companies that trade crypto through indirect Multi-Level Marketing (MLM) principles. Let's call them "Crypto Poolers" or CP

There are literally hundreds of CP companies. For example, quite a few CPs will ask you for an initial investment anywhere between $100 and $25,000 or more. You were probably invited by a "sponsor" or someone that invited you to watch a free Zoom seminar or YouTube video. In these video meetings the presenters are so excited, saying things like "this is the newest breakthrough!". They also show you fancy charts, how the profit works or a pretty passive income structure calculator. How the CP makes money is they are essentially pooling money together to invest in crypto and then providing you with the return. These returns are not guarantees and experts consider these types of investments in the high risk category.

Some CP's are legit, especially if you get in early and pull your returns out early. Like I mentioned earlier, I have several friends that live by these types of CP companies right now and have become millionaires. However, some companies are scams and many of my friends have lost lots of money.

Please do your research. There so many companies that claim to be professional crypto currency platforms, with artificial intelligence, or bots that scan crypto currency and this AI software makes the best decision on what coins to buy. Many of them are legally registered to be a crypto traders. Again, mainly what they are, are "poolers" who have gotten together, created a trading platform and start asking for your investments through MLM like concepts.

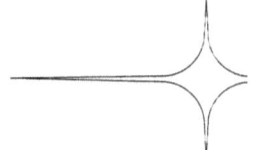

For example, I send you a zoom link/invite and say it is an opportunity to make passive income via crypto. You then invite 10 of your friends and they all invest $1000. I now receive $10K. Of course as my "invitee" you get a cut or commission from brining your friends into this opportunity. Then I tell you all about my company, say I am a crypto expert and a legit crypto trading platform company. Then behind the scenes, I use that money to trade crypto or another platform like Forex. I then pay you back in returns to your "crypto wallet" that you have set up so that you can withdraw to your bank account.

Now I will ask you this- why couldn't you create a company just like that on your own? Humm! Good question. I still invest in crypto. However, I pay very close attention to my money and each company to which I give my money. Again, some of these companies are super legit. Others are scams. Do your research.

My job in this book is not to discourage you from trading crypto or even encourage you to put all your eggs in one basket, but to explore the numerous potential income streams while working your 9 to 5 or if unemployed, earning income without having to spend a lot of capital. With crypto currency just like with any other investment vehicle, you need to invest money, monitor it's growth, sell when necessary, buy more when the opportunity is right and diversify when necessary. This is especially important when it comes to stocks and more specifically monthly dividend stocks.

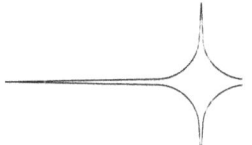

SECTION 5
WEBSITE AND MOBILE APPLICATION DESIGN

QUALIFYING FACTORS	GRADE
Difficulty Level (DL)	2.5
Realistic Earning Potential (REP)	$1 - $1500 Per Month
Monetary Investment (MI)	Medium
Potential Time Commitment (PTC)	2-4 hr/per/day
Suggested Marketing Structure (SMS)	Paid

I chose web and mobile app design as a way or earning online because it was a good source of income for me. I did website and mobile app design all while working a 9 to 5. From there I moved into real estate a few years ago and was able to work from the comfort of my home. When it comes to website and mobile app design, you don't have to know any coding (although this does not hurt at all to know some). You just need to know how to communicate and be a project manager. The key word here is "outsource". When I was earning my MBA, that word outsource along with globalization were key phrases during my years in grad school. I have used outsourcing for years and yes, it works. Because I have been doing websites and mobile apps for a while now, I did decide to take a few courses on coding as well as how to build mobile apps on specific app building platforms. I have found that this added knowledge only helps me to better communicate the needs of the project and to better manage the project. However, I still outsource most of my work.

Because most businesses (small to large) have and need either a website or an app, or updates, new features added or fixes to a web or app related problem, there will always be a need for website and mobile app development. This is still big business. There are 2 ways to do this:

1. Take a website or mobile app development course on Udemy or some other teaching platform so that you can build sites and apps yourself; or
2. Outsource all of your work and become a very good project manager.

#1 is self-explanatory so I'm not going to get technical with that. Just know that learning a new skill can be very valuable in the short and long run. And when I say valuable, I also mean that literally because you can save money by performing tasks yourself. Yes, you will be expending your time but those are things to weigh to determine what works best for your strategy.

For #2, as I stated above, when it comes to outsourcing web/mobile app development, you have to be a good communicator. Here's how the outsourcing can work. Essentially, you advertise your web designer or mobile app developer services on social media, and send people to your website and/or how to contact you. You then outsource the job to the freelancer developer that you hire. The key is to manage this project for your client closely and precisely. With the knowledge you gain from learning how to build websites and mobile apps, you will be able to provide this excellent service to your clients.

Again, everything on how to build websites is online. There are several web-building platforms. At the end of this Section I include a short list of them. On some of these sites, you can even resell the hosting services for a small recurring fee. Let's look at a more realistic example. I will share my personal experience with you so that you can have a realistic view of the process.

My friend Samantha was starting a small business where she rented ATM machines to local brick and mortar startup businesses. She needed a website. I charged her $400 initially for the a WordPress site build-out and this price included a seven page website, special features including custom data forms and other content gathering features, and a 20 minute video tutorial (outsourced) that showed her how to manage her site. I also charged her $12 per month for the hosting. The entire job took two weeks to complete.

Here is what I did - I found a good WordPress template to use on ThemeForest.com for $50. I hired a freelancer through a freelancer website (Upwork.com) and paid them $10 per hour to work only 20 hours per week. Here's the part most people won't tell you. Because I already knew how to communicate with overseas freelancers and some knowledge of WordPress, I understood that it would not take them more than 10 hours to build a 7-page website on WordPress. If the freelancer responded that it would take longer, I'm definitely not hiring that freelancer. After an import of the demo site (which already contained most pages from ThemeForest.com) the developer was able to complete the full website, content and all, in less than two weeks.

Here's an overview.

- Charged - $400
- Freelancer - $10 per hour for 10 hours = $100
- ThemeForest.com Template - $50

Total Profit $250

So if I had 10 clients that's $2500 earned in two weeks. Please take into consideration that I have been doing this for some years now so the flow was easy. All of my clients were referrals which came through word of mouth, so I didn't have to advertise. As I have mentioned throughout this book, your time is also valuable because time is also money. So my total time spent talking to the client and freelancer, making changes, updates on drafts, etc. totaled 4 to 6 hours over the course of those two weeks.

Again, please do your research and please take time to learn a new skill on every platform you choose. Learn how to communicate well with international freelancers if you use them and learn how to be a good project manager and planner.

Tip - When hiring freelancers, weed them out. Ask them questions about their communication style, their turnaround times on projects similar to yours and ask them to give you an estimated number of hours that it will take to complete your job. Most good developers, even the ones that ask for very little per hour, can build WordPress fully responsive and interactive websites in under 6 hours tops. Most of these developers have the technical skills to do that. Here is the list of website building sites as promised above. I don't necessarily recommend the GoDaddy or Wix type websites. I suggest building sites on more open source content management systems like WordPress. However, you can use which ever open source platform you choose. There's a ton of information on YouTube, articles and blogs about building sites.

Here's a list of the mostly used free open source website building platforms:

	NAME	WEBSITE	INFORMATION
1.	WordPress	wordpress.com	According to WordPress, 42% of the entire web is built on WordPress. Probably. Very popular and comprehensive platform for website building
2.	Drupal	drupal.org	Very easy to determine your website development needs as they break a lot down by industry and specific website needs
3.	Joomla	joomla.org	Recently released its latest version and constantly updates its tools for efficiencies.
4.	Plubii	getpublii.com	One of the newer website building platforms that claims simple and accessible website creation regardless of skill level.

Important note: You will need a domain name and a hosting plan from a company like GoDaddy. If you find your first choice for your website name is taken or costs an exorbitant amount to purchase, try variations of your desired website name. Also, I suggest securing the .com, .net. .org, .co, etc. of your website name. The following are companies to consider:

	NAME	WEBSITE	INFORMATION
1.	GoDaddy	godaddy.com	By far, the most popular place to search and secure your domain name. Customer service representatives are extremely knowledgeable and helpful.
2	HostGator	hostgator.com	Has been in this game since 2002 so very reliable hosting company. Many experts place HostGator as the best overall web hosting service on the market right now.
3.	SiteGround	siteground.com	Excellent WordPress for speed and security.

Mobile App Development

It's my recommendation that you at least take a course on Udemy on using one of the below platforms if you're going to jump into mobile app design. Please note that some of the best mobile app building platforms are:

- Flutter
- React Native
- Xamarin
- Ionic Framework
- Cordova

Some of them are crossplatform applications meaning that they are used for both iOS and Android type phones.

Flutter is an open-source and free mobile software development kit (SDK) that is effective in developing native-looking cross-platform applications. It will help you produce creative mobile applications for Android and iOS platforms with the same codebase by using a modern and reactive framework.

React Native created by Facebook (Meta) is a popular JavaScript-based cross-platform framework that can let you develop effective natively rendered applications for both Android and iOS platforms.

Xamarin is a C# based framework meant to develop effective cross-platform applications, and it is a Flutter similar framework.

Ionic framework is an open-source SDK designed for easier cross-platform application development. The first version of this framework was developed in 2013, based on Angular JS and Apache Cordova.

Cordova is another useful application development framework rebranded Nitobi and released this framework's open-source version.

SECTION 6
REAL ESTATE

QUALIFYING FACTORS	GRADE
Difficulty Level (DL)	3.5
Realistic Earning Potential (REP)	$5K – $30K Per Month
Monetary Investment (MI)	Minimal
Potential Time Commitment (PTC)	2-4 hr/per/day
Suggested Marketing Structure (SMS)	Paid

Real Estate is big business and there are so many different ways to earn from real estate even without having a license. Millionaires are made every day in real estate. There are so many books, blogs, YouTube videos and a ton of information on how to earn and operate a successful real estate business. Although, there are a slew of other forms of earning with real estate such as Fix and Flip (and in some instances no credit is needed), Rental Properties and much more.

Because this is a book about earning income or having multiple income streams all online while working from home, I'm only going to share one small aspect of real estate that can earn you money online while working from home. This is real estate wholesaling. Wholesale real estate involves the following process- you directly contact a home owner to buy their home at a fairly low price. Once you have contracted with the home owner to purchase their home, you sell that contract to an investor or cash buyer, of course for a higher price in order to make a profit. Once the contract is settled and the investor or cash buyer remits payment to you, you then remit to the home owner the agreed upon selling price. The deal is done. Ultimately, you're selling real estate contracts. Wholesalers act as intermediaries between sellers and buyers, who are usually investors. A wholesaler will usually contact owners of distressed properties or any property that seems to be a good deal for an investor. A good deal for all means the following:

a good profit for the home owner; a good profit for you; and an eventual good profit for the buyer/investor. What is most important to the buyer/investor is the after repair value (ARV). You as the wholesaler are in a unique position to have to know what will be good for all parties involved. This means understanding the current value of the property and what the owner may still owe on the property if anything. This means understanding how the property can be repaired and rehabilitated and the value of the property after this is done. This means understanding what that value could be and listing the right price to potential buyers/investors. This means understanding the market in the area so that your pricing makes sense for all involved.

Let's look at a quick example of a wholesale deal. Raymond's Dad needs to be moved to a nursing home and he needs to sell Dad's property. The house needs some repair. Ray is unsure what to do with the property. Wendy is a wholesaler and notices in the property tax records that the owner contacts have changed. (This could be a clue that an owner is looking for a hassle-free way to get rid of the property.) Wendy decides to make an offer on the property for $90K and close in 30 days or less (with wholesaling, emphasis on the "or less").

Ray is relieved to not have to put the property on the market, go through an agent and broker, fix up the home, fill out mounds upon mounds of paperwork, etc. Raymond agrees to sell. Wendy then gives Ray an assignment contract (please see a lawyer for these types of contracts in your State) and Ray signs the contract. Wendy then sends out an email blast to her cash buyers list along with pictures of the home and a detailed description of the home such as this:

- Asking Price: $100k – Buyer to pay all closing costs
- After Repair Value - $200k
- Supporting Comps (comparable) to other homes in the area (these would be listed)
- Other important information about the property

A cash buyer decides to make an offer to Wendy for the asking price. Wendy then accepts the offer and then the property is sold through a professional title company and Wendy collects $10K for the sale.

Many wholesalers develop their own strategies for finding sellers of homes and then their own strategies for finding and soliciting to a cash buyers to buy the home. I'm not going to get too deep into wholesaling strategies right now mainly because each strategy will depend on your local market conditions and there are numerous strategies and combinations of strategies that will work for you depending on your geographic area of choice and the real estate industry at the time you engage in wholesaling. However, here are a few:

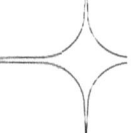

- Cold Calling (you can purchase lists, hire companies to cold call, etc.)
- Bandit Signs
- Social Media Marketing
- Direct Mail
- Driving for Dollars (canvassing neighborhoods with distressed properties)

Pros and Cons

Pros

Wholesaling real estate can be done with very little up front capital even if you have no credit or a bad credit score. No investment is needed and wholesaling real estate does not require you to buy and hold properties or find financing. It can all be done from the luxury of your own home. Most wholesalers will go personally to see the home before they make an offer and do a ton of research before making that offer as well to ensure they are going to have the best deal in order to sell that property quickly. But caution- do not think you have time on your hands in the wholesaling business. Wholesaling is popular in many markets so, the real estate industry is a "time is of the essence" industry which means real estate contracts must be completed as soon as practicable without undue delays. You can also outsource most of your marketing strategies and in some cases not even leave the house. For example, you can hire someone to see, examine and take pictures of the house for you. There are even people you can hire now that will try to close the deal for you but all for a fee, of course.

Wholesaling is good money. It can be a large amount of money. For example, a typical one time wholesale deal can profit you anywhere from $3K per sale up to $25K per sale. If you can close 2-3 deals in a month, you can see how that income builds very quickly. Many real estate investors have started off with wholesaling and then move into investing after building up a substantial amount of capital from wholesaling.

Cons

Saturated markets. I'll say it again. Saturated markets. In some cities and states, the wholesale market is saturated with so many hungry entrepreneurs trying to get a taste of building capital through wholesaling. What that means is that many home owners have been bombarded with tons of emails, mailings, calls, door knocks, etc. from wholesalers making offers on their homes. So if you call, knock, mail or email, what makes your offer any different? Your marketing strategy will need to stand out and this strategy may require some paid marketing services.

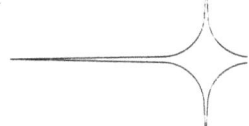

It's very important with wholesaling to develop a good buyers list. Depending on how much risk is written for you into the contract with the seller, you may lose the deal if you do not get a buyer in time. For this reason, it is best to have buyers in mind before initiating an offer to the home owner. This will not only lessen your risk of losing money should a buyer not come through, but will also ensure that you have a good reputation as a wholesaler.

One major downside of wholesaling is that success is never guaranteed. You could find your first deal within a week, or you could go months without coming close. You will likely face plenty of rejection before you find a deal, which can be discouraging. No one wants to sell their home for a super low price, so you will have to be patient to find a truly motivated seller.

In many cases, some sellers are typically in a bad financial situation or have recently gone through a difficult life situation such as a divorce or recent death. As a result, they can often be emotional or under a lot of stress. You will need to learn how to be gentle and caring when dealing with these types of potential sellers because you don't want to take advantage of someone's misfortune. You must be patient and sympathetic to their situation, or the deal could fall apart.

Finally, most wholesalers make dozens or even hundreds of phone calls before they find a potential lead, and even then, the deal could still fall through. So be ready to hear a hundred no's before you hear that one yes.

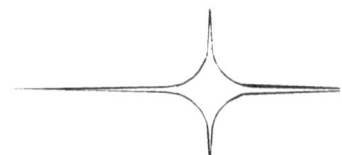

SECTION 7
REMOTE WORK
(WORK FROM HOME)

QUALIFYING FACTORS	GRADE
Difficulty Level (DL)	1-3
Realistic Earning Potential (REP)	Minimum Wage - $450K+
Monetary Investment (MI)	Minimal
Potential Time Commitment (PTC)	Average 10 hours/week - 80+ hours/week
Suggested Marketing Structure (SMS)	Grassroots

As we are all aware, the way we "do work" has changed drastically since 2020, the start of the pandemic. People either learned how productive they could be by remote working, or companies learned that maximum productivity can be realized outside of the traditional office setting.

At the outset, remote work can mean:

- Working from home in a full time or part time position;
- Working from some other location in a full or part time position (but not in a traditional office);
- Working from home or another location a number of days in a week and in a traditional office setting the remaining workdays (commonly known as telework);
- Any combination of the above.

Remote work opens many more opportunities for companies to seek out and hire qualified individuals who normally would not apply for positions for various reasons. Geographic location is no longer a barrier. Available hours to work is no longer a barrier. Inability to relocate is no longer a barrier.

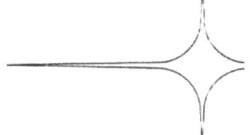

Further, individuals who are experiencing more unique situations can find something that fits their schedule. Stay-at-home parents can find positions that allow them to work during nap times, during the hours that children are at school or during later evening hours. Family members who are caring for their parents and loved ones have a greater opportunity to attend to their parents' needs and earn income during not-so-traditional working hours and days. Then there are individuals who have full-time positions but need supplemental income. These people can seek out positions that will fit their full-time schedule and perform the remote duties at home.

Years ago I had a part time position in an office. The position did not require full time working hours but this worked out for me because of my obligations to family at the time. However, I knew I needed some additional income so I looked into positions that allowed me to work from home whenever my schedule would allow. I started doing transcribing work for a company that did court cases. I was able to choose how much work I did and when I could. Some weeks, I spent 10 hours transcribing and other weeks I only spent two. It all depended on my personal schedule and availability.

There are a ton of major companies that will hire you to work directly from home. Big brands like Apple, Target, Hulu, etc. will pay you to promote their companies. Go online to their career section and search for remote jobs.

As a strategy, because these remote jobs are flexible with your schedule, some people are able to incorporate 2 to 3 of these additional jobs into their regular 9 to 5 schedule and earn upwards of $50 to $200 per day from each job. If you take that top number which is $200 and multiple that by 3 additional jobs, you can earn an additional $600 a week. Keep in mind that this may require quite a few working hours. However, it could lead to very comfortable high earning income levels.

Pros and Cons

Pros

The Pros of remote work can seem pretty obvious. For example, remote work means less time, or no time, commuting in traffic, spending money on gas and wear and tear on your vehicle. These are hours that you can commit to your work time at home or a location close to your home. There are also benefits such as not having to spend as much money on business attire and even on breakfast or lunch outside of the home as when you are working in an outside office. The overall work-life balance of remote work just cannot be beat.

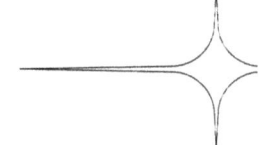

Cons

However, there are some Cons. Some companies do not treat you as an employee but instead as a contractor or 1099 worker. This means companies will not provide a health benefits package (which can include health, vision and dental) and financial benefits package (which can include retirement/pension and 401K type accounts, and life insurance). Companies also do not have to perform your withholding functions for Federal and state taxes and social security. Please take these items into account when you are calculating the amount of income you will receive. The items just mentioned will become expenses subtracted from your remote work income received. Finally, due to the nature of some levels of remote work, you may not accrue sick and vacation leave. Therefore, when you find yourself not able to work due to a sickness, medical appointment or even a vacation, you will not be compensated for the time you are not working.

Below are just a few examples of where to find remote work positions. Of course, this is not an extensive list, but I give my pros, cons and views on them all.

	NAME	WEBSITE	INFORMATION
1.	FLEXJOBS	flexjobs.com	Pros – Area of specialty is remote work and hybrid positions. Employers can find you. Dedicated team that pre-screens positions to ensure legitimacy. Cons – There is a cost to sign up to access the repository and apply for positions.
2.	Remote.Co	remote.co	Pros – Good selection of remote positions. You can apply through the website or your LinkedIn account. Cons – Search only allows to one level, e.g. you can search for legal positions but cannot narrow that search to Legal positions that are part time. You are either searching all legal positions or all part time positions.
3.	Just Remote	justremote.co	Pros – Claims to have access to the 70% of remote work positions that are not posted on "other" websites. Just Remote claims that because of the costs to post jobs on websites, companies only post 30% of their job openings. Cons – Their search engine, "Power Search", costs $6 to access. Power Search is how to access the 70% of unlisted job openings.

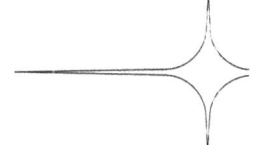

4.	WorkingSolutions	workingsolutions.com	Pros – An established company that has short term and long-term contracts with corporations to provide customer service. You do not have to seek out companies yourself to provide. Cons -This is not a job search engine website. It is a company that you have to apply to in order to work for them to provide customer service to other corporations. The work and therefore pay could be sporadic. You are working for a company that holds contract with other companies. If the client decides to not work with WorkingSolutions any longer, you would be out of work until WorkingSolutions finds another client for which you can work.
5	NexRep	nexrep.com	Pros – Similar to WorkingSolutions, this is an established company that has short term and long-term contracts with corporations to provide customer service. You do not have to seek out companies yourself. Cons -Also, similar to WorkingSolutions, this is not a job search engine website. It is a company that you have to apply to in order to work for them to provide customer service to other corporations. The work and therefore pay could be sporadic.

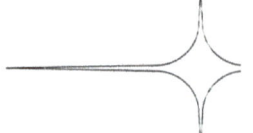

SECTION 8
DROP SHIPPING

QUALIFYING FACTORS	GRADE
Difficulty Level (DL)	4
Realistic Earning Potential (REP)	Approx. 15%-20% of sales Average of $700 week (high level of time commitment to average this amount)
Monetary Investment (MI)	Medium
Potential Time Commitment (PTC)	40+ hours a week
Suggested Marketing Structure	Grassroots - Paid

Here's one way of how this works - You create a page on social media, a website landing page or even a virtual brochure. You search your supplier's inventory (see list below for a few of the favorites) for products that you think will sell like hotcakes. You put those products on your page, list a price and advertise. When an order is placed, the supplier fulfills the order (or you send the supplier the order to fill) and the supplier ships the product directly to the buyer. You have entered the world of drop shipping. In essence, you become a vendor of the actual manufacturer or retailer who originally sales the product. Some of the top sites to conduct your drop shipping business are Shopify and Amazon.

Do not look at the "glamorous" side of what I stated above. This all takes extremely hard work, commitment, and your time. To make drop shipping work for you, you must be dedicated. Approximately 10%-20% of drop shipping businesses are actually successful. But if you have what it takes, then go ahead and be a strong part of that 10%-20%!

Drop shipping has its pros and cons and those are listed below. Be mindful of spending thousands of dollars to take an online course on how to become a drop shipper. There are legit paid drop shipping programs/courses out there that will

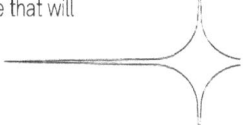

genuinely teach you. If you find that you just cannot commit to a thorough Google or YouTube search to educate yourself on the topic, then just beware of those online courses and seminars that claim to have the inside scoop and even private lists on drop shipping opportunities. Some great resources of how-to information can be found at Shopify, Amazon and Oberlo, just to name a small few.

It is very possible to conduct your drop shipping business in a manner where you not only establish a clientele base but you also gain the trust of the original manufacturer/retailer. Let's be honest, if your site is so popular that it provides additional exposure for the manufacturer/retailer and their sales are increasing, they can only appreciate your business and work harder to make sure you succeed. Further, if you are providing top notch customer service to buyers, you will continue to experience repeat buyers who will seek out your site for products they are looking to purchase.

Pros and Cons

Pros
- NO INVENTORY! Enough said.
- No shipping activities or costs.
- You do not need a super expensive complex website with multiple pages and listings of products.
- Depending on the site, you may not have to deal with any customer service issues.

Cons
- You have no control over the inventory or supply chain.
- Products may not be what they are advertised as. Because you are relying on the quality of the products based on the original manufacturer/retailer claims, you are responsible if the buyer does not receive a satisfactory product. For example, that red dress in the photo with a description of quality cotton or silk may be a faded pinkish cheapened material dress when it gets to the buyer.
- You could be liable for products that are defective, delayed shipping and even trademark issues (unless you have an iron clad contract in place with the original retailer relinquishing all liability).
- You may have to deal with your buyers for customer service, the good and the bad.

Here are some of the top drop shipping suppliers:

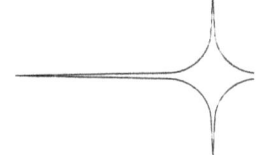

	NAME	WEBSITE	INFORMATION
1.	Wholesale2b	wholesale2b.com/index.html	Some might disagree with me on placing this at #1. However, if you are a US based drop shipper, and considering that Amazon has completely changed the time-for-delivery game, consumers may not want to wait 6 weeks for their product. Wholesale2b is US based and therefore shipping can be as short as a one day turnaround. It is the primary reason it is at #1.
2.	Sunrise Wholesale	sunrisewholesalemerchandise.com	Similar to my #1, this is at #2 for the same reason- lower shipping times.
3.	Wholesale Central	wholesalecentral.com/index.htm	Wholesale Central lands a top spot also because of its US-based shipping. However, this site is free and boasts of 700,000+ items.
4.	Modalyst	modalyst.co	I like this site because it is tailored towards more high end products. It also has at its disposal (and thus at your disposal also) AliExpress which has millions of products from which to choose.
5.	World Wide Brands	worldwidebrands.com	World Wide has been in this business for over 20 years. It completely understands the Business 2 Business (B2B) standard so you will definitely find full, all-around business support with World Wide.

Obviously missing from the above list is Alibaba and AliExpress. They are both discussed in detail in *Section 2 Your Brand Using Alibaba*.

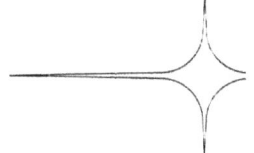

SECTION 9
HOSPITALITY/LODGING RENTAL

QUALIFYING FACTORS	GRADE
Difficulty Level (DL)	1-5
Realistic Earning Potential (REP)	$250 - $2,500/week
Monetary Investment (MI)	Minimal - High
Potential Time Commitment (PTC)	1 – 60 hours/week
Suggested Marketing Structure	Grassroots - Paid

The hospitality industry, or short term rental industry, has changed significantly in the past 10+ years. That change is primarily due to one company- Airbnb. Currently, Airbnb has over 6 million listings in 200+ countries. However, Airbnb was technically not the first popular company to offer vacation and temporary rental listings for individuals looking to rent their properties on a short-term basis. Vacation Rentals By Owners, more commonly known now as Vrbo, began helping homeowners list their personal properties in 1995. Vrbo, now owned by Expedia Group, boasts over 2 million listings in nearly 190 countries. While they are competitors, I tend to view Vrbo as the higher scale Airbnb. I believe Airbnb has also bought in to this view, but it has not stopped them from bringing innovation and niche ideas to the company. Airbnb now touts its "Airbnb Experiences" where vacationers can go beyond just searching for a home away from home for a vacation but can actually vacation with a theme. There are at least 2 ways to earn from short term rentals:

1.   Rent your own property on Airbnb.com or other similar site
2.   Sub-Lease

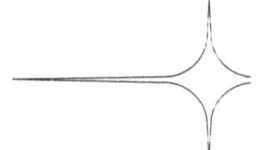

Rent Your Own Property – Sites like Airbnb and Vrbo provide all of the guidance and help that you will need to take your property or even a room in your home and turn it into a money-earning venture. Depending on your property, location, space, etc., you can earn anywhere from $250/week to $2500/per week or more.

Sub-Lease – If you are currently renting your home or apartment, be careful. You must adhere to the language in your rental or lease agreement as it regards subletting. If the legalities of subletting works in your favor, you're all set. You are ready to use the sites listed below and begin earning additional weekly income. A young lady that I know rented a 3 bedroom, 2 bathroom apartment in New York. She lived in two of the rooms but that empty third bedroom was just sitting, not brining any value to her already very expensive monthly rent. She decided to rent that third bedroom through Airbnb and essentially earned the equivalent of her monthly rent for the entire apartment in just a couple of weeks of Airbnb'ing that one bedroom.

If you choose to offer your home, rental property or even the extra room in your home on your own and without the likes of an Airbnb or Vrbo, there is much to consider. I highly suggest that you seek legal counsel so that you can rent your property for short-term rental purposes in a safe manner where you are protected legally and understand your responsibilities and liabilities. It is very involved so seek professional guidance.

Now, to my Valuation Table above. There is much to explain with the range of numbers and calculations of each valuation. Let me break this down.

The DL encompasses the full range. If you own your property/have full rights to the property, if this property is in a prime vacation location where demand is high, and if you contract out for all of your services including cleaning, security and management, then your DL is a firm 1. As you move closer to the hands-on management and upkeep of your property and find that your property is not in a prime vacation or high event location, your DL moves to a 5. It will just take more work on your part to make your listing is as attractive as possible.

The above also plays a part in your REP. A 4 bedroom, 4 bath, multi-level home with a game room and private pool with beach access to the hottest beach or directly across from a major theme park can yield thousands of dollars a week. At the same time, this exact same home in a more secluded suburban neighborhood 75 miles from the center of vacation life might bring just a few hundred dollars a week. Because there are so many variations of rentals from number of bedrooms and baths to proximity to attractions and entertainment, the earning potential is measureless.

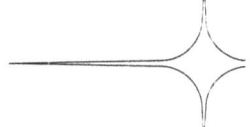

Your MI can also vary drastically depending on what you currently own and can legally rent out/sublease. There are people who own an extra home already or rent their own home during certain seasons. Their initial investment may be anywhere from a cleaning crew to a general contractor to do property fix-ups. If you are wanting to get into the short-term rental/vacation rental industry and you do not own property, well of course your initial investment will be the entire purchase of a home or property and everything involved to have it ready for renting.

As mentioned above, depending on your level of management, your PTC could be as little as 1 hour per week to check in with your property managers or as high as 60 hours a week if you have multiple properties for which you are the manager and engaging in every activity from cleaning the properties between guests to yourself providing such activities as Personal Concierge services for the guests at your properties.

Finally, your SMS can also vary. You can simply post your listing(s) on Airbnb and/or Vrbo and let your property and reputation (from guest ratings) be your marketing tool or you can actively advertise your properties across social media and other marketing outlets.

	NAME	WEBSITE	INFORMATION
1.	Airbnb	airbnb.com	Airbnb has mastered the short-term rental/vacation market. As an Airbnb Host, you will receive everything you need to ensure that you can rent your property and be protected. They offer everything from $1M in insurance to reservation screening to 24-hour safety support.
2.	Vrbo	vrbo.com	I have to admit, these are only ranked because of apparent popularity. But Airbnb and Vrbo, while in the same general industry category, are actually very different. And I appreciate the differences. Vrbo and their wonderful marketing and advertisements boasts vacation rentals for large families to create memories. As stated above Vrbo stands as a more "high-end" choice for short-term and vacation rentals.

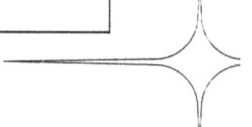

3.	Booking.com	booking.com	Booking.com is not just for flights and notels, although that is clearly what the site is most known for. But the website has great listings for vacation and short-term rentals under the site categories of "apartments", "resorts", and "villas".
4.	TripAdvisor Vacation Rentals	tripadvisor.com/Rentals flipkey.com holidaylettings.co.uk(UK) niumba.com (Listings in Spanish)	TripAdvisor has a completely separate website (and websites) for its listings. It is actually a tab under the regular TripAdvisor website. The site has rental property listings in over 200 countries around the world.
5.	Expedia	abritel.fr (France) fewodirekt.de(Germany) bookabach.co.nz (New Zealand) stayz.com.au (Australia)	This entry lists Expedia because Expedia owns all of these vacation rental sites in these countries. Impressive… and so are the listings. Just make sure you can speak these languages (save Australia) or use a translation tool so that you don't book a 2 bedroom flat when you need a 10 bedroom mini mansion.

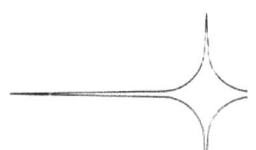

SECTION 10
MYSTERY/SECRET SHOPPER

QUALIFYING FACTORS	GRADE
Difficulty Level (DL)	3
Realistic Earning Potential (REP)	Average of $25/hour(Free product or service plus small fee - $100+ per assignment)
Monetary Investment (MI)	Minimal
Potential Time Commitment (PTC)	5 - 40 hours/week
Suggested Marketing Structure	N/A

Companies use mystery or secret shoppers (we will use secret shopper here) to gather information on the overall customer service experience at their business locations. Companies are trying to determine the quality of the experience their employees provide a customer while at their locations. Companies also use secret shoppers to determine what is missing from the customer's experience and how to improve the overall atmosphere and even layout of their locations.

Secret shopping can range from a very light level of time commitment to nearly consuming your entire day. For example, I did quite a few secret shopping assignments for a national oil change company. This company claimed to get you "in and out" so my mission was to observe the time, customer service, safety and efficiency of the process. My time commitment here was less than an hour, I was reimbursed for what I paid for the oil change and compensated an additional $35. Not that bad for an hour. However, I did a secret shopping assignment where I visited a car dealership and in order to observe and assess all that the company needed me to, I ended up spending nearly 3 hours in that car dealership! The compensation was pretty nice however, as I was paid $125 for basically sitting in nice cars with the new car scent and listening to a salesperson drone on and on about the particulars of torque and the range of city and highway mileage.

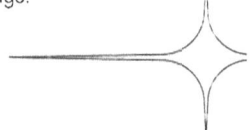

Also understand that your time commitment as a secret shopper does not end when you leave the establishment. You have to provide the company the actual feedback! This involves using whatever online tool the company maintains for their secret shoppers to provide their feedback. So for the examples above, you can add approximately 15 – 45 minutes to that time commitment.

As a secret shopper you will very likely need access to a car depending on the assignment, where you live and where the assignment is located. If you are a big city dweller with no car, there are numerous opportunities for assignments, for example, major retailers in the city. Additionally, please understand that some assignments require you to purchase a service or products up front. You will be reimbursed according to the instructions with the assignment, however, and then paid the secret shopper assignment fee on top of that.

Finally, please heed this **WARNING!** – watch out for scammers! If you are ever solicited to be a secret or mystery shopper via mail, it is likely a scam. You may also be solicited to be a "customer service evaluator". Same thing. These scammers will send you a letter explaining what you have to do, claiming they represent a marketing or advertising company working for a major retailer or corporation. They will also send you a check for several hundreds to several thousands of dollars. Your instructions are to deposit the check into your bank account and then wire the scammer a certain amount of that money. You are then to keep the remainder of the money to use to shop for when you conduct your evaluation. Of course, the check is fraudulent but by the time you wire money from your own bank account to these scammers, the check has been returned to your bank and you are out of your personal money. You end up incurring fees and issues with your bank and possibly an investigation into depositing a fraudulent check.

Here are a few reputable companies that work with reputable corporations for YOU to contact about becoming a secret shopper. Note that I do not break down the pros and cons of these resources because in this industry, the pros and cons are very specific to the individual and the types of assignments you wish to take.

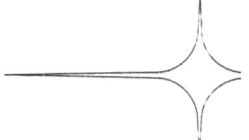

	COMPANY	WEBSITE	INFORMATION
1.	BestMark	bestmark.com	BestMark has been in business nearly 37 years. Zero chance this company is a scam. Their reputation is steller. Other similar opportunities include Intercept Interviewers (capturing customer feedback when customers leave a store or business) and Compliance Auditors (reviewing company safety, regulatory, policy, etc. guidelines). Mystery Shoppers Providers Association (MSPA) Member.
2.	The Elite CSX Group	elitecxs.com	Veteran-owned business that has a personal touch when it comes to shoppers. Remember, their business is customer service, so they have to be great at it themselves. Mystery Shoppers Providers Association (MSPA) Member.
3.	IntelliShop	intelli-shop.com/how-to-become-a-mysteryshopper	Very reputable company. You have the opportunity to get some of the best assignments based on your personal ratings from previous assignments.
4.	Market Force	marketforce.com	Focuses primarily on retail, food services and hospitality companies.
5.	Mystery Shopping Service	mysteryshoppingservice.com	This business has been around for over 23 years. Their industry of focus is senior living and healthcare, real estate, retail and hospitality.

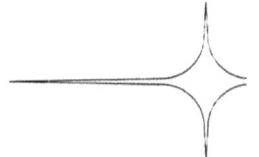

SECTION 11
INFLUENCER

QUALIFYING FACTORS	GRADE
Difficulty Level (DL)	3
Realistic Earning Potential (REP)	Average of $25/hour(Free product or service plus small fee - $100+ per assignment)
Monetary Investment (MI)	Minimal - Medium
Potential Time Commitment (PTC)	5 - 40 hours/week
Suggested Marketing Structure	N/A

It is amazing to me how an "average" (I don't like that word but it helps you get my drift) person can make a post about an opinion or something funny and go viral overnight. And yet there are others who post purposefully in an attempt to go viral. These individuals share their post with as many of their friends as possible. Those friends share with their friends and the next thing you know, boom!, Jerry has hundreds of thousands of likes and just as many new followers. Please read **Building A Following** in **Section One** which talks about sharable content. See also the end of this Section to learn how to monetize in these instances also.

At this point, Jerry can count this 15 minutes of fame as a win and keep living. Or Jerry can see this as an opportunity to spend the next years of their life dedicating a good portion of their day to preparing for and actually posting their ideas and opinions. An Influencer is born.

Just when I think, my goodness there are a gazillion people on this social media app and no one can still be getting a million+ followers, I find yet another "new face" that has punched their way through the increasingly addictive universe of social media and made their mark. From teeny-boppers to wise-old baby boomers and older, influencers are steering the way we think about ideas, products, and services. AND, they can be compensated for it all. Of significant note, and not at

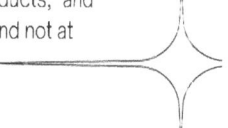

all surprising, the highest number of social media users are millennials (about 85% of them) and Gen X'ers (about 75% of this group).

So outside of the "lucky chance" that a random post of yours goes viral and you capitalize off of this 15 minutes of fame, how exactly can you become a social media influencer? First and foremost, you must have a following. Again, see **Building a Following** in **Section One** for strategies on growing your followers. As you are building that following (or once you have that following) make sure that your posts are creative, engaging and shareable as mentioned in Section One. In your posts, mention a product or service and use your hashtags for these products and services. Mention a company and give reviews on that company or their products and services. This is a great way to get noticed by these companies and brands. Additionally, there are ways for you to put yourself in front of companies looking for influencers. For example, Izea.com and Collabstr are basically "talent agencies" of sorts for influencers and companies looking to hire influencers for marketing purposes. But I will say it again, you must have that following. When I was looking for influencers to promote one of my companies, the first thing I looked for was people with the certain amount of followers to better help promote my company.

There are several ways to be compensated as an influencer. You can be compensated with the actual product or service that you are mentioning, or you can be paid money. Monetary payment can be a one-time flat fee, an ongoing contractual fee for posting about the product or service at some frequency (e.g. once a week), or payment can be calculated based on how many sales a company receives as a result of your post.

Now you may find that you are an overnight sensation or you may already have a following but note that in the universe of social media influencing, these numbers below are important to companies as to whether or not they will "book" you and for how much. The following is not an exact science, even down to the number range of followers, but it is a solid guide to help you understand.

- **Nano Influencer** – as a Nano you will have a smaller following of around 1,000 – 10,000 people. But do not let the smaller numbers be a discouragement-companies are sometimes more likely to reach out to the Nanos because a smaller following could mean greater engagement in your posts resulting in greater engagement with the company or brand you are promoting. Nanos are also less likely to be influencing a ton of other products or services causing yours to get lost in the mix.

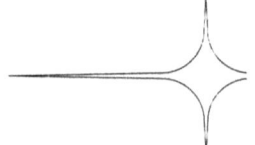

- *Micro Influencer* – as a Micro you are likely to have between 10,000–50,000 followers. As a Micro you might be considered more of an "expert" on the topics, products and services that you promote and discuss. Micros are likely to have a strong niche.

- *Macro Influencer* - as a Macro, you're getting into the big leagues at this point and have a following between 40,000 and 1 million. You may not be seen as an expert but depending on the demographics of your followers, you may be exactly the person a brand or company is looking for.

- *Mega Influencer* - you are ruling social media if you have 1 million+ followers and you are considered a Mega Influencer. Some brands find this attractive because apparently anything you say gets attention. This might be a great way for the brand to reach new customers. As a Mega, you are commanding high monetary compensation and this very well might be your only source of income needed to maintain a financially fruitful lifestyle.

Before determining which social media platform(s) will be best for you to influence, research even deeper on the demographics and marketing/advertising aspects of each of these. The following are not listed in order of best sites for anyone to use. My descriptions offer more insight for you to determine the most important aspect of being an influencer- your audience. Know your audience.

	COMPANY	WEBSITE	INFORMATION
1.	Instagram	instagram.com	If your target audience is 18-40-somethings, Instagram is a great choice. Users ages 18-34 make up over half of Instagram's users. A downside of Instagram is the inability to put links in posts. You can mention any product or service you are promoting in your posts but any links to them will have to go in your Bio. On Instagram, however, #HashtagsRule.
2.	TikTok	tiktok.com	TikTok is quickly becoming an all-ages social media outlet. The demographic of users looks like this- over 90% of its users are aged 13-34. That's a wide range of individuals and products to influence. TikTok videos just catch people's attention these days. Let's be honest – wordy posts don't have the same impact as a video that can "speak" the same words.

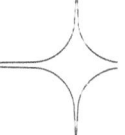

3.	YouTube	youtube.com	Definitely the most used site to learn "how-to"... anything. It is technically the second most used search site (behind Google, of course). YouTube boasts users of all ages from toddlers to seniors. YouTube, however, tracks its users from age 16. But honestly, all of that does not really matter here. Point blank, YouTube has BILLIONS of users every day, every minute of the day of all ages, stages, likes and dislikes. You cannot go wrong with a YouTube page but because of its vast popularity, you will have to invest intelligently in marketing yourself/your page on YouTube.
4.	Facebook	facebook.com	THE most used social media platform. However, you are not reaching any tweens and teeny boppers on Facebook. Their parents? Yes. The majority of Facebook users are ages 18-54 making up over 70% of its users. Those 65+ however have also caught Facebook fever in recent years. The lure of Facebook is that you can post it all- words, pictures, videos, links, songs, etc. and your posts can be as short or lengthy as you please.
5.	Twitter	twitter.com	All of the latest "who owns the company" and "what's up with that guy" news aside, Twitter allows for much of what Facebook does but most notably with character limits. Consider Twitter like a blog and even better, a blog that is good for on-the-spot feedback and responses to posts. Users are primarily between the ages of 18-49 accounting for nearly 60% of Twitter users.

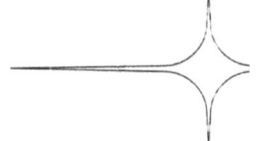

BONUS SUBSECTION ON YOUTUBE

This bonus section is worth your time and worth the special shoutout to YouTube because YouTube is unique in these aspects below. You can earn money on and through YouTube in several ways. Of course, first you must have a YouTube account and page so set that up if you do not currently have one. Make sure the name of your page is catchy and reflective of what you are trying to do. You will also need a Google AdSense account. If you already have an AdSense account you can just connect it to your YouTube account. Let's explore.

YouTube Partner Program – This is THE way to get paid through YouTube. You will sign up through your account and by clicking on YouTube Studio. Under *Other Features* choose *Monetization*. This is where you will create or add your Google AdSense account. Select your preferences and you're ready. If you want to estimate how much you can earn, then from your Dashboard choose *Analytics* and then *Revenue*. Under *Monthly Estimated Revenue* you can determine what you can earn and incorporate your strategy (from all those tips and tricks in the Section One) to make it happen. Remember the importance of building your following and a great way to do that is to make sure every video has at least one "call to action", that is, telling your audience to do something. You've heard this before… "if you like this video don't forget to hit the like button and subscribe"!

Once you have built your following, created great, relevant and sharable content, consider the YouTube Premium Program to increase your potential earnings. YouTube Premium is a membership program that your subscribers and other watchers can sign up for to watch your content without ads. How do you earn from this if this is a membership with YouTube? You will get paid from YouTube based on how much and how often subscribers to this membership program watch your content.

Finally, of course through your YouTube page you can generate other ways to earn income and some of these include selling merchandise through posted content (make sure to trademark your logo used on your merch), advertise your other business(es) if you have any (e.g. affiliate marketing), add links in your video descriptions (to your merch, other businesses), etc.

License to Content Media – We have all seen how viral a video can go, right? Well, if your video goes viral, you can earn money from that viral video. Technically you do not even have to set out to make it go viral or create content with the purpose of it going viral. You've seen these videos, e.g. where a mom posted a hilarious response to her child solving a math problem about money or an attorney showing up to a virtual court hearing with the face of a cat. (If you haven't

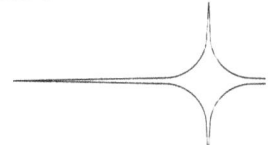

seen or heard of these viral videos, do a quick YouTube search right now for some comic relief. Thank me later.) Viral videos such as this end up on national morning shows, the news, everywhere.

Well, as the "creator" of these videos, you can license your content to these news outlets and others who may be interested in using it for news stories, their ads, etc. Your license, their use, you get paid for it. There are also online sources (e.g. Trusted Media Brands) that act as brokers or marketplaces that list such videos where you can include yours for more possibilities of monetizing your viral videos.

Creative Commons License Program - This is something that you can do whether or not you create content on your own YouTube page. That's right. You do not need to produce one video to license content media through YouTube. It's simple-re-use other YouTuber's content. It's totally legal so don't worry. YouTube has an entire library of sorts of videos that they have included under their "Creative Commons License" program. You get a license to this library of videos which allows you to publish other creator's content and then earn money from those posts. What's more, you can edit and tailor the video however you want (within the confounds of YouTube's policies) and essentially make it your own. You would need to follow the steps noted above for making sure you get paid through your YouTube account with your Google AdSense account.

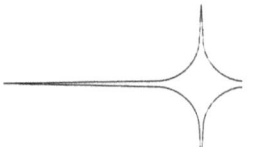

SECTION 12
RESALE PERSONAL ITEMS

QUALIFYING FACTORS	GRADE
Difficulty Level (DL)	4
Realistic Earning Potential (REP)	Varies
Monetary Investment (MI)	Minimal
Potential Time Commitment (PTC)	1 - 10 hours/week
Suggested Marketing Structure	Grassroots

92 million tons of fabric waste is produced each year. That's one trash truck every second dumping nothing but clothes into landfills. Most items returned to a retailer (for any reason) end up in landfills to the tune of over 2.6 million tons. Clothes can take up to 40 years to decompose and shoes can take up to 1,000 years to breakdown. And I will not even get into the greenhouse emissions and water waste that results from the fashion industry every year. So why not properly recycle your clothes, shoes, handbags, and other accessories... and earn money while doing it?! Over 95% of textiles can be recycled in some manner. Hopefully these astonishing numbers have inspired you to check out the resources below to, well, essentially save our planet AND earn some money in the process. Oh and by the way, over 70% of the world wears secondhand clothing so there is definitely a market for those clothes and shoes in your closet gathering dust.

The clothing/apparel resale industry is HUGE! And I mean that for both sides of the sell. There are tons of people selling their items online but there are also tons of consumers looking for these items. As a seller, you have to make yourself stand out and you do this by utilizing some of these strategies:

- Make your posts attractive and creative. Do not just take a bland picture of your clothes, shoes and jewelry. Use backgrounds, check your lighting and even use friends or yourself to model the items.

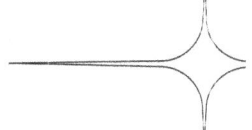

- Offer to pay for shipping or tell buyers that if they pay the asking price for your items, you will cover the shipping.
- Offer a "free" item if someone purchases a certain amount of items (e.g. 3 or more) or their total purchase amount meets a threshold amount (e.g. $100).
- See other strategies in the table below specific to the websites listed.

There are companies that operate as online consignment shops but I will not be discussing those here. (Remember, this book is about you earning additional income and a credit for your gently used items to purchase "new" items, while a very honorable idea, is not the same for the purposes of this book.)

	COMPANY	WEBSITE	INFORMATION
1.	Poshmark	poshmark.com	Poshmark is a convenient app where you create your account and upload photos and descriptions of your items. This app has millions of items on it so you will have to be pretty good at marketing your items. Poshmark offers a great way to do this by hosting "parties" amongst the app users. You can join other users' parties or create one yourself and invite users. This will give more visibility to your items.
2.	Facebook Marketplace	facebook.com/marketplace	Although Facebook Marketplace may be mostly known for households items, furniture, bikes and even cars, you can also sell clothing here. As with these other sites and apps discussed here, the Marketplace is flooded with users and items so you will have to standout with great photos and very, very competitive pricing. The biggest downfalls with the Marketplace is there is no buyer protection and usually the sells require a face-to-face meet up... with a stranger. However, there is nothing stopping you from offering to mail items to the buyer.

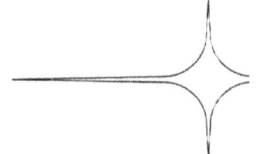

3.	Depop	depop com	Depop is very similar to Poshmark in terms of creating your account on the app and posting appealing photos of your items. This app also has millions of items on it so you will have to be pretty good at marketing your items and navigating through the app amongst the other sellers and buyers to get noticed.
4.	The RealReal	therealreal com	The RealReal deals in luxury brands. Drop off, ship or schedule a pick up with their White Glove service. They will sell your items for you. When items sell, you can opt for direct deposit or site credit (i.e. consignment). The RealReal also has 18 physical locations in the U.S.
5.	Vestiaire Collective (formerly Tradesy)	us vestiairecollective com	Verstiaire Collective is for higher end and designer clothing. It uses an app where you can upload photos of your items to list. Once they sell, you ship them to Vestiaire where they will authenticate the and handle the rest. As with the others, there is a fee for selling your items with Vestiaire.

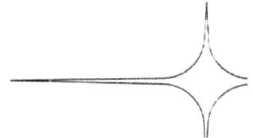

SECTION 13
VIRTUAL TEACHER
(YOU DO NOT NEED A DEGREE OR LICENSE)

QUALIFYING FACTORS	GRADE
Difficulty Level (DL)	3
Realistic Earning Potential (REP)	$250 - $2,000+/week
Monetary Investment (MI)	Minimal
Potential Time Commitment (PTC)	3 - 20 hours/week average
Suggested Marketing Structure	Grassroots and Paid

It does not even have to be explained how the COVID pandemic changed the landscape of connecting virtually. These virtual connections truly opened wide open the door for learning beyond the classroom for both children and adults. Virtual learning not only supplements educational curricula (e.g. tutoring) but also allows for learning outside of the traditional education system (e.g. learning a new language or discipline).

What is even better is that virtual learning has no borders. You can be in the United States and help a student in India improve their grades in Statistics. You can be in China and help an adult in Argentina learn Mandarin. The possibilities are endless. You just have to know the resources you need to be successful at this growing area of learning.

Organization is the key with virtual learning. You must understand each of your clients, their current level of understanding in the subject(s) you will instruct and their goals by the end of your instruction sessions. Also note that your clients can be across time zones so you will have to structure your days around their schedule, their "waking" hours. You could be helping someone learn at 3:00am in your time zone.

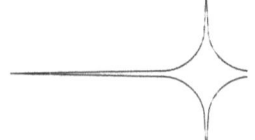

If you are already a teacher and you have a "traditional" school year where you have around two months in the summer without having to teach, virtual teaching is such a great way to earn additional income as convenient to your summer leisure hours. However, if you have a 9 to 5 or other income streams, virtual teaching allows you to utilize your own skills and experiences to teach others or create videos to offer on a one-time purchase or subscription basis. The video route, I can say, is a good way to earn additional income. I purchased a subscription to one of the websites I mention below so that I could learn how to create mobile applications on iOS and Android. I was able to purchase the subscription and work at my own pace to learn this skill. I also know people that were traveling or relocating to another country and needed to learn the language in that country. They were able to take live virtual foreign language lessons.

The below resources are great places to start your search on how you will build and grow your virtual learning business. And remember, you can teach courses across any one or more of the platforms offering virtual learning.

See also **Section 9 Remote Work** for additional resources for finding virtual learning opportunities.

	COMPANY	WEBSITE	INFORMATION
1.	Wize	wizeprep.com	Wize is one of the many, many online teaching platforms out there. However, Wize does not charge a fee for you to use its platform and further it does not take any fee from your delivered courses! Wow. Wize connects you the tutor/instructor with students all across the country.
2.	Udemy	udemy.com/teaching/	Udemy has a very similar platform to Outschool (below) but its reach goes far beyond elementary and secondary students. Adults all over the world sign up for Udemy courses every day and you can be an instructor with Udemy to tap into that following. Udemy also offers for you to teach in various manners, i.e. live or recorded courses and offering courses in increments.

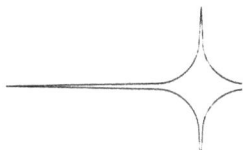

3.	Outschool	outschool.com/teach	Outschool has a very unique model where it allows anyone with the expertise (or even passion) in a subject area to offer their courses online. Certifications are not required as Outschool believes that adults can impart their knowledge to students based on their experiences and interests. There is a criminal background check and you must be a citizen of the U.S., Canada, Australia, New Zealand or the U.K. It does not cost for you to list your courses but once you get paid clients, Outschool will swipe 30% of that for their fee. Outschool also works with schools so your reach could go beyond individual clients.
4.	TeachAway	teachaway.com/online-teaching-jobs	Online search tool and website for you to specifically find opportunities to teach subjects online. The majority of the positions require teacher or a certification of some sort to qualify.
5.	Verbling	udemy.com/teaching/	One the most comprehensive formats to teach and learn a new language is Verbling. This site is not just for students who need additional assistance with their foreign language subject in school but also for other learners who need to learn (for job, business, etc.) or who just desire to learn a new language. You must have experience in that language and be a native speaker of that language to join Verbling.

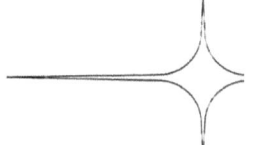

REFLECTIONS

&

ADDITIONAL RESOURCES

REFLECTIONS

I wrote this book in the hopes that you as the reader would become educated on the many, many ways to supplement your current income or even replace it with these resources. I also wanted to give you more than just a list of websites where you could click and search. I wanted to equip you with strategies, techniques and tools so that you could maximize these opportunities to best fit your skills, schedule and lifestyle.

With any of these opportunities I want you to remember the importance of viewing your venture into these opportunities with serious professionalism. Create and properly incorporate your business. Remember the tax implications of your additional streams of income whether or not you find it necessary to create an established business to engage in any of these opportunities. With the majority of the Sections in this book, you will need to ensure that your system is in place. Your system will determine your level of success in any business venture you pursue. Without a firm system in place you will certainly find yourself just chasing money and wearing yourself out just to make sure you get it. A business system is when you have a business that operates and (more importantly) earns profitable income while you sleep, without having to indulge 60 hours of labor hours actually working the business.

Finally, I hope all the success to you in all of your endeavors. I want you to take everything that I have said in this book to propel you and your ability to make your lifestyle exactly what you want it to be. If you wish to take these opportunities and your business to the next level, check out my *Additional Resources* below. Thank you for spending this time with me by reading my book.

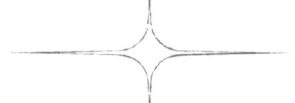

ADDITIONAL RESOURCES

I offer services in the following areas if you need direct help. If you're serious and ready to invest in your future and learn how to create a business system, you can go visit the link below and someone will contact you:

ReprogramMyMind.com

Business Structure Consultation
Website and Mobile Application Development Consultation
Real Estate Consultation
Legal Contract Consultation
Marketing Consultation

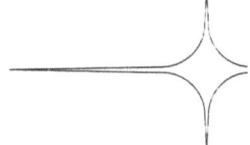

MY
NEXT
STEPS

www.ingramcontent.com/pod-product-compliance
Lightning Source LLC
Chambersburg PA
CBHW072334290526
45794CB00002B/868